THE AMERICAN FILM HERITAGE

IMPRESSIONS FROM THE AMERICAN FILM INSTITUTE ARCHIVES

THE
IMPRESSIONS FROM
AMERICAN
THE AMERICAN FILM INSTITUTE
FILM
ARCHIVES
HERITAGE

By

TOM SHALES

and

Kevin Brownlow

Robert Cushman

John Davis

Joseph E. Dispenza

William K. Everson

Tom Flinn

Bruce Henstell

Kathleen Karr

Lawrence F. Karr

Leonard Maltin

David L. Parker

Burton J. Shapiro

David Shepard

Joel E. Siegel

Paul Spehr

David Thaxton

Pamela C. Wintle

Stephen F. Zito

Foreword by

GREGORY PECK

 Published by **ACROPOLIS BOOKS LTD.** Washington, D.C.

Acknowledgments

The American Film Heritage was edited by Kathleen Karr, with the assistance of Sali Ann Kriegsman, Sam Kula, David Shepard, and Stephen F. Zito. The introductions were written by Tom Shales.

In the preparation of this book, The American Film Institute gratefully acknowledges the assistance of the contributing authors, the staffs of The American Film Institute and the Library of Congress, and especially Sarajane Johnson and Pamela C. Wintle.

The American Film Institute is indebted to hundreds of individuals and institutions whose cooperation and public spirit have made possible the acquisition of more than 9,000 American motion pictures for permanent preservation in the AFI Collection at the Library of Congress.

A national film preservation program in America is now being pursued by AFI Archives, The Museum of Modern Art, George Eastman House, and the Library of Congress, with support from the National Endowment for the Arts. The program is guided by AFI's Archives Advisory Committee: Sam Kula (AFI), Chairman; Edgar Breitenbach, John Kuiper (Library of Congress); Eileen Bowser, Willard Van Dyke (Museum of Modern Art); James Card (George Eastman House); film historians William K. Everson, Arthur Knight, Andrew Sarris; Chloe Aaron (National Endowment for the Arts), ex officio.

The American Film Institute, George Stevens, Jr., Director, is an independent, non-profit organization serving the public interest, established in 1967 to advance the art of film and television in America.

The American Film Institute, The John F. Kennedy Center for the Performing Arts, Washington, D.C. 20566.

ACROPOLIS BOOKS LTD.
Colortone Building, 2400 17th St., N.W., Washington, D.C. 20009

Printed in the United States of America by
COLORTONE PRESS Creative Graphics, Inc., *Washington, D.C. 20009*

Design by Stephen Kraft

Library of Congress Catalog Number 72-3813
International Standard Book Number 87491-335-7 (cloth)
336-5 (paper)

Frontispiece: *An early attempt to achieve color effects through tinting and toning. E. K. Lincoln and Hope Hampton in THE LIGHT OF FAITH, 1922.*

Foreword

The widespread recognition of the significance of motion pictures in American life is a fairly recent phenomenon, and to many people it is still a revelation that the films of their childhood had a value beyond the entertainment of the moment. It is a sad fact that this recognition has come too late to save more than half of the films produced in the land renowned for the development of this vibrant 20th Century art.

Despite the vigorous efforts of private institutions such as The Museum of Modern Art and George Eastman House to select and acquire outstanding films in the past thirty years, a combination of producer indifference in an industry which never had the leisure to look back, and the self-destructive nature of the nitrate film itself, took its toll. The films of the past, masterpieces and program features alike, disappeared from view or disintegrated in studio and distributor vaults as the films passed from hand to hand.

This book reflects a new national effort, initiated by The American Film Institute working in collaboration with the Library of Congress, The Museum of Modern Art, George Eastman House and other organizations, to locate and preserve the films that have survived. The key element in this new program is the support of the National Endowment for the Arts, which estab-lished the Institute in 1967, for film preservation is a very costly undertaking that is beyond the limited resources of private and non-profit organizations. As a member of the National Council on the Arts, which advises the Endowment, and as Founding Chairman of The American Film Institute's Board of Trustees, I take pride in the emergence of a coordinated national program for film preservation as a major step in facing up to the years of neglect.

The American Film Heritage is not a history of the American film. As its subtitle indicates, it is a series of impressions based on an examination of a collection that is itself, of course, only part of our film heritage. The American Film Institute Collection, and the other collections that are benefiting from this program, are conserving the essential raw material on which future histories of the American film will be based. That history is now being rewritten as forgotten masterworks are rediscovered. What we are gradually learning at the same time is that the films also have significance as historical and sociological documents. They retain the power not only to delight us, but to enlighten us as well. As art and as history, they are being secured and preserved as a valuable part of our cultural heritage.

Gregory Peck

List of Contributors

KEVIN BROWNLOW is a filmmaker, film historian and the author of *The Parade's Gone By*, published by Alfred A. Knopf, Inc.

ROBERT CUSHMAN is a Research Associate of The American Film Institute completing work on the career of Mary Pickford.

JOHN DAVIS is co-author, with Tom Flinn, of *Michael Curtiz*, published by November Books.

JOSEPH E. DISPENZA is Education Programs Manager of The American Film Institute.

WILLIAM K. EVERSON is a film historian and author of numerous books on the cinema, including *The Western: From Silents to Cinerama* (with George N. Fenin) published by Orion Press, and *A Pictorial History of the Western Film*, published by Citadel Press.

TOM FLINN is co-author, with John Davis, of *Michael Curtiz*, published by November Books.

BRUCE HENSTELL is Publications Coordinator of The American Film Institute's Center for Advanced Film Studies.

KATHLEEN KARR is a Cataloger with *The American Film Institute Catalog*, published by R. R. Bowker

LAWRENCE F. KARR is an Associate Archivist of The American Film Institute.

SAM KULA is Archivist and Assistant Director of The American Film Institute.

LEONARD MALTIN is the editor and publisher of *Film Fan Monthly* and the author of several books on film including *The Great Movie Shorts*, published by Crown.

DAVID L. PARKER is Technical Officer of the Motion Picture Section, the Library of Congress.

TOM SHALES writes on the arts for *The Washington Post* and reviews films for National Public Radio.

BURTON J. SHAPIRO is a Cataloger with *The American Film Institute Catalog*.

DAVID SHEPARD is Theatre Programming Manager of The American Film Institute.

JOEL E. SIEGEL is the author of *Val Lewton: The Reality of Terror*, published by Viking Press, and is working on a study of Vincente Minnelli.

PAUL SPEHR is Motion Picture Specialist of the Motion Picture Section, the Library of Congress.

DAVID THAXTON is an Associate Archivist of The American Film Institute.

PAMELA C. WINTLE is Archives Assistant of The American Film Institute.

STEPHEN F. ZITO is Editor of *The American Film Institute Catalog*.

Table of Contents

Introduction
Moving Image/American Image

Annabelle doing her Serpentine Dance in Edison's "Black Maria" studio, 1894.

Annabelle danced, the suffragettes marched, President McKinley talked, and America's love affair with the movies was under way. Through laughter and tears, both on screen and off, the affair has endured for over seventy-five years, with the moving image reflecting the American image and changing with the times.

From the earliest days in nickelodeons the movies found their audience, and it was, perhaps, because the popular response was so immediate and so widespread that custodians of culture took so long to recognize that the entertainments were also social and historical documents. And it was almost half a century before the archons of academia discovered that the toy had become an art and was worth protecting and preserving.

The credit for the invention of cinematography has at least four serious claimants in as many countries, but they all have one thing in common. When they first succeeded in placing a continuous strip of celluloid in an intermittent camera movement so they could create an illusion of continuous motion, what they focused on was real people doing what they do where they normally do it. These primitive fragments of reality—newsfilms and actualities that constitute a moving record of people and places—are a legacy of the invention of cinematography, and in America it was a legacy that was so neglected, it is only by accident that any have survived.

Not only were the actualities and the first attempts at narrative films ignored by those whose task it is to archive the present and record the past, but the moving images were fixed on strips of nitrocellulose, a flexible and long-wearing but chemically unstable and dangerously flammable compound. It is as if every book in the Library of Congress were printed on paper that would self-destruct and disappear forever unless copied every five or ten years.

To the Library, which had been accepting paper prints (35mm strips of photosensitive paper on which the films were recorded frame by frame) for copyright registration since 1894, the problems of storing nitrate seemed insoluble; and when changes in the Copyright Act allowed the producers to deposit nitrocellulose copies, instead of paper prints, the films themselves

Dr. Shaw in a suffragette parade in Washington, D.C., from a 1910 newsreel.

had to be rejected. For over three decades the Library returned the films to the producers and distributors, and in an industry where the films were regarded as product, yesterday's output could be discarded or allowed to disintegrate when there was no longer any demand in the marketplace.

When The American Film Institute was established in June, 1967, more than half the films produced in the United States prior to 1950 were no longer known to exist in any form. (Safety film, a non-flammable and relatively stable acetate stock, became the standard in the industry by 1952.) Preservation of films produced in the nitrate era is a race against time, in which the rules of the game are not at all precise. Nitrate film has been known to survive under stable conditions of temperature and humidity for as long as seventy-five years, but it sometimes shows signs of serious decomposition in only a few years, particularly if it has been improperly processed or stored under extreme conditions of temperature and/or humidity. The film literally disintegrates over time, so

that the container may be found to hold only a sticky roll whose images are dissolving or, at a later stage, a lump of dried out nitrocellulose turning into brown powder.

The Institute's first concern was to preserve the vanishing heritage—whether entertainment film, actualities and documentaries, or newsfilm—for the archival efforts of the Library of Congress, The Museum of Modern Art, and George Eastman House had already demonstrated the cultural value of all kinds of films. The Institute's role, with the support of the National Endowment for the Arts, has been to stimulate and coordinate a national film preservation program, and to create a national collection at the Library of Congress comparable to the national collections of cultural artifacts at the Smithsonian Institution.

Concentrating its resources on acquisition and preservation, the AFI established The American Film Institute Collection at the Library of Congress as an integral part of the national collection. This guarantees the security of the films while the Library assumes the responsibility for storage, maintenance, and reference services. Like all films in the national collection, whether acquired by gift or by deposit as evidence of copyright registration, the films in the AFI Collection are thus legally the property of the United States Government. Exhibition and duplication for use outside the Library is dictated by the owners of the copyright and/or the donors of the physical property where these exist.

All the films in the AFI Collection are, however, accessible to students and scholars on the premises of the Library, subject only to the existence of reference prints. In this way the AFI is pursuing the first two objectives of the archive program, and has achieved them in relation to the films now in the AFI Collection: to assure the preservation of significant American motion pictures and to provide access to this material for students and scholars. A third objective is to make the Collection available to the general public through specialized exhibition or the regular channels of distribution.

The primary intent of the Institute's archive program is to secure and preserve significant American films

President McKinley giving an address in 1897.

which represent the growth, development, and maturity of an important art form. The search here is not only for great films but for films which reflect advances in filmmaking techniques and mark stages in the careers of important filmmakers.

A second, but no less important, intent is to secure and preserve films for their content, for their value as sociological and historical records. The Institute's archivists recognize that because films reflect the social milieu in which they are produced, capture attitudes and opinions of the time, and record the changing nature of American society, they constitute a rich resource for students and scholars in many disciplines. It is a platitude to say that "all films teach," but it is a fact that every film makes a conscious or unconscious statement about the values, mores, and societal relations of the characters who appeared in them, the people who made them, and the audiences who watched them. The films in the AFI Collection, therefore, range from the acknowledged masterpieces of the American cinema to relatively obscure "program features." The Collection also includes documentaries of little artistic value but whose content constitutes an important record, and newsfilm preserved for subject content alone.

In the pages that follow, we present some impressions of the AFI Collection. There is no attempt here to be either definitive or comprehensive; the great films and the great names included in the Collection but not discussed here are legion. What follows is essentially a sampler of the kinds of films we are attempting to acquire and safeguard in the public interest. The approach is somewhat idiosyncratic. We asked the staff and our colleagues in the field to comment on aspects of the Collection about which they were knowledgeable and interested. The results vary from a scholar's meticulous description of early color techniques to a learned enthusiast's appreciation of the comedy short. Along with these varied observations on aspects of the Collection, we asked Tom Shales, a perceptive young critic, to appraise a dozen films selected from the Collection almost at random.

An underlying theme in many of the articles is "preservation"—a term which requires careful defini-

tion for archival purposes. Some of the films described in these pages were long believed to be "lost." No copies were known to exist in studio vaults or museum and archive collections. Working through an elaborate network of private collectors and our contacts abroad in the International Federation of Film Archives, we managed to secure preservation copies of many of these films for the AFI Collection and the nation. Many more of the titles mentioned in these pages have never disappeared from view—they are readily recognized as staples of late-night viewing on television or in the inventories of 16mm non-theatrical distributors. They could be said to "survive," but as the years pass what "survives" is a pale shadow of the original. The Institute's effort in these cases is to secure good quality 35mm prints or preprint material (negatives or fine grains), as close as possible to the original. With rare exceptions, television prints are not only many generations removed in optical and sound quality from the original, but they also suffer from censor cuts and distributor trims so that the films will fit into allotted time slots.

Perhaps the most dramatic examples of survival are films that must not only be recovered but must be restored through diligent archival efforts. Three examples should indicate the complexity of the work: THE POWER AND THE GLORY, in which an incomplete negative and sound track acquired from the studio was completed by material from Preston Sturges' own copy; THE FRONT PAGE, where the film with a poor sound track was acquired from a foreign archive, and the sound track added from Vitaphone discs loaned by a private collector in San Francisco; THE EMPEROR JONES, which was pieced together from several surviving 16mm prints, a few feet, and sometimes a few frames at a time.

We do not believe this book reflects all of the variegated riches of the AFI Collection, but we do believe it suggests the value of this resource for interdisciplinary studies beyond film art alone. A true appraisal of film as a cultural artifact is a full scale study in itself. But we hope this book will help make clear the extent to which the moving image is part of America's cultural heritage.

An example of nitrate disintegration: park police dismounting and mounting for Edison's camera in 1896.

MISS LULU BETT

Famous Players-Lasky. 1921.
Director: William C. de Mille.
Adaptation: Clara Beranger, based on the novel and play by Zona Gale.
Cast: Lois Wilson, Milton Sills, Theodore Roberts, Helen Ferguson, Mabel Van Buren, Clarence Burton.

Lois Wilson and Clarence Burton in MISS LULU BETT.

Almost everyone has heard of Cecil B. De Mille. He was hard to ignore. But for every Cecil we know, there's a William we don't know—in this case, Cecil's brother, whose work was largely ignored for forty years. Film preservation can help to correct such oversights, and the eight de Mille features acquired from Paramount Pictures and now in the AFI Collection give us a chance to look closely at the work of a formerly unsung artist. Others await their rediscovery.

William de Mille's identity is largely eclipsed, not only by the scarcity of surviving prints, but by the exceedingly luminous career of his younger brother Cecil B. Cecil differed from William in many ways—the most superficial of them being that Cecil spelled De Mille with a capital "D" and William employed the lower case. Superficial—but symptomatic. Where Cecil was given to the grandiose, William preferred the intimate. Where Cecil was known for his hellfire and brimstone—both on the screen and on the set—William was softer-spoken, easier-going, and perhaps more humanistic. MISS LULU BETT, one of William de Mille's surviving films in The American Film Institute Collection, displays these qualities to perfection.

Agnes de Mille, William's daughter and a famous choreographer, talked about the differences between her father and her uncle to Kevin Brownlow for his book on silent films, *The Parade's Gone By* (Alfred A. Knopf, Inc., 1969).

"Cecil was operatic," she said, "whereas William was more interested in human values. He was concerned with humor, and with half-light, with the psychological states where emotions are mixed and graduate one into the other. He was absorbed by the characters of ordinary people. . . .

"On father's set it was always quiet. They called him Pop. . . . Pop wore a battered old hat which he would never give up. He wore it for thirty years. He always looked rumpled, and he slouched around and spoke very quietly. If he became angry, it was a quiet and powerful anger. . . . Father was normally very patient and very intimate. . . . Cecil spent his life building up a legend. Father was interested only in the truth."

Lois Wilson and Clarence Burton in MISS LULU BETT.

Brownlow himself writes of William de Mille on the basis of MISS LULU BETT as having been "a man of great warmth and perceptiveness. He cared more for psychological reality than melodramatic action, and his style was as different from Cecil's as a miniaturist's from an epic painter." Of the film itself, Brownlow says, "de Mille's compassion and his realistic treatment give every scene a truthfulness still rare in the cinema. It retains its magic, and this fragile, delicate little story can still move its audience to tears."

MISS LULU BETT does indeed reveal a talent of subtlety and sensitivity. The film is relatively free of the posturing and exaggeration that plagued much of the silent cinema. Griffith's greatest weakness, perhaps, was the cloying saintliness of his heroines—a vision of virginity that must have seemed incredible even in its own time. De Mille's heroine, Miss Lulu Bett, described as a "timid soul" in the titles, is nevertheless a believable character—a three-dimensional woman. De Mille's film has emotional power, yet it refuses to wallow in sentiment. It is alert to the small details that define characters and relationships, and the director was able to convey them with delicacy and tact. In an era of overstatement, he managed not to say too much—but rather, just enough.

The screenplay for MISS LULU BETT was written by Clara Beranger, who was de Mille's wife, and there is obvious harmony between the written film and de Mille's interpretation. De Mille was a writer himself. Before going to Hollywood, he'd written such plays as "The Warrens of Virginia" and "Strongheart." He also wrote screenplays for his brother Cecil, including "The Woman God Forgot" and "Temptation." And he helped Cecil launch a wave of semi-sophisticated sex romps in the twenties with WHY CHANGE YOUR WIFE? (1920), starring Gloria Swanson and Bebe Daniels. Apparently, de Mille himself thought the genre had definable limits. He is quoted as having cautioned, "It would never do to have the Virgin Mary getting a divorce, or Saint Joan cutting up in a nightclub." Anything else—or almost—went.

MISS LULU BETT is a film that reflects genuine care and attention to detail. Beranger adapted it from a novel and play by Zona Gale. Lois Wilson plays the role of Miss Lulu Bett, described in the titles as "the family beast of burden, whose timid soul has failed to break the bonds of family servitude." She lives with her sister, brother-in-law, and mother in an all-American household; that is, something of a mess. Her brother-in-law, Dwight Deacon (Theodore Roberts), is a pompous oaf; his wife is a supplicative ninny (Mabel Van Buren) who calls him "Dwightie." An older and a younger daughter and Lulu's mother also contribute to the household miseries.

The film establishes its theme—but doesn't really summarize itself—with the three opening titles: "The greatest tragedy in the world, because it is the most frequent, is that of a human soul caught in the toils of the commonplace. . . . This happens in many a home where family ties, which could be bonds of love, have become iron fetters of dependence. . . . If you want to know what kind of family lives in a house, look at the dining room."

The first shots in the film, of course, are of the dining room. The family is then introduced. Lulu is first seen working at the family stove. It quickly becomes apparent that Miss Lulu Bett is a virtual slave in the house—because she has nowhere else to go. When Dwight's brother Ninian (Clarence Burton) returns home from South America after twenty years and takes the family to dinner, he laughingly goes through a mock marriage ceremony with Miss Lulu Bett. It seems like just a tasteless joke until the father declares, "Say, we forgot I'm a justice of the peace," and the marriage is therefore valid. For lack of something better to do with her life, and for the hope of getting away from the oppressive Deacons, the girl decides she might as well be married, even to this dude. The marriage ends—Ninian, it turns out, already was married to someone else—and Lulu is faced with the humiliation of returning home just seven days later. But "for a whole week," note the titles, she knew "the joy of having someone treat her kindly," and this will eventually contribute to her liberation, when she asserts her independence, leaves the Deacons, and at last rewards the amorous advances of stalwart schoolteacher Neil Cornish (Milton Sills).

Liberation is somewhat the theme of the film (today it might be called "The Liberation of Miss L.B.").

17

Coincidentally, Miss Lulu raises one of the issues of semantics lately advanced by Women's Lib when she first meets Ninian:

He: "Is it 'Miss' or 'Mrs.'?"

She: "'Miss.' From choice. What kind of a Mister are you—a 'Miss Mister' or a 'Mrs. Mister'?"

He: "That's right—a man's name don't tell you if he's married, does it?"

Let the records show that the issue came up in 1921.

Throughout the film, Lois Wilson's performance, under de Mille's alert direction, conspicuously avoids the pathetic. The role might indeed have turned into a cross between Cinderella and Little Eva. But when Lulu announces at one point, "I still have my pride," we believe her, because she, Beranger, and de Mille have given the character dignity.

Similarly, the Deacon family, though hardly a collection of heroes, isn't a set of stock villains, either. De Mille stops short of making them too onerous. Small things contribute to the portrait—as when father insists that dinner is late until his watch is proven wrong by the 6 o'clock factory whistle sounding in the distance. He claims then that the whistle must be wrong, that it's a trick to get more work out of the men. We recognize in this behavior the symptoms of common pomposity—not villainy.

Peripheral details are helpful, too. At the city restaurant, a quartet of high-lifers stir their drinks with flower stems—a fresh image of affluent decadence. When a local suitor named Bobby plans an elopement, de Mille catches the panic all over his face. When the elopement attempt is thwarted (by the clear-thinking Miss Lulu Bett), Bobby remembers to cash in the two train tickets he will no longer be needing. De Mille's treatment of the burgeoning romance between Lulu and the schoolteacher is deft and non-cloying. At the end of the film, in the teacher's classroom, a student has scrawled, "Teacher loves L---" on the blackboard. To show Lulu how he feels—still maintaining a discreet distance—the teacher completes the sentence, and then writes, "Does Lulu love me?" She writes the letter "Y" and, before she can complete the word, they kiss.

Crucial also to the film is de Mille's sense of period Americana. It permeates the interior scenes at the Deacon house, but surfaces most notably in a scene outside the church on the Sunday after Miss Lulu Bett has returned from her unsuccessful marriage. The subject of the sermon has been "charity of heart," but as soon as they're out the door of the building, the women and men divide into groups and gossip. "Her husband got tired of her and sent her home," jabber the women. "If a feller leaves his bride after one week, it don't say much for the bride," gloat the men. The teacher stands up to this small-town Puritan ritual by offering Lulu a ride home in his crank-up car. The women scoff that men invariably chase after "a woman who ain't regular." The sequence conveys something sanguine about provincial mores and basic middle-class values.

The whole film conveys a great deal. And one of its most obvious revelations is that William de Mille may be one of the true unsung poets of the silent screen. When film preservationists can contribute toward the restoration or overdue establishment of a reputation like de Mille's, they perform a service both to the art and to the artists. William de Mille was, from available evidence, just such an artist.

"Blazing Technicolor," "Stunning Trucolor," and "Shocking Eastmancolor"

David L. Parker

Like almost everything else, the technical evolution of the movies did not happen in a simple, orderly way. It took trial-and-error experimentation to arrive at an industry standard for sound. Tussling over a standardized aspect ratio continues to this day. And the means of filling a film image with color have been many and diverse. Film preservation offers an opportunity to trace not only the aesthetic and sociological milestones (and detours), but also the technical, physical changes that film has gone through—a history both complicated and, more to the point, colorful as well.

Figure 2. Leatrice Joy and E. A. Warren in
A TALE OF TWO WORLDS, 1922.

Although it is commonly believed that films in color began with the introduction of full-color Technicolor in the middle thirties, from the outset there have been three kinds of color films, and examples of these may be found in The American Film Institute Collection and other collections in the Library of Congress.

As early as 1895, New York City audiences saw movies that had been colored by hand. The Edison Kinetoscope Company in their film of ANNABELLE'S DANCE attempted to simulate the effects of the colored lights which played over her body during her stage performance by hand-coloring the black-and-white pictures frame by frame. A print of this 1894 film in the collection of the Library of Congress has her white dress hand-painted in half a dozen different colors.

By 1907, Pathé Freres was applying color mechanically, by the use of stencils, one cut for each color, then retouching by hand. The colors, though sometimes charming, were limited in number and in realism, but, thanks to them, a Pathé film such as DOWN IN THE DEEP (fig. 1), could offer pink fairies rising from blue sea froth, green whales, and heroes in gold armor, an effect so striking that it was remembered from his childhood movie-going by the Russian director Sergei Eisenstein.

The practice of hand-coloring a part of the black-and-white picture persisted as late as 1922, as can be seen in the red-painted heart in a print of Cecil B. De Mille's melodrama, FOOL'S PARADISE. Because the rest of the frame is without color, the colored part

Figure 1. DOWN IN THE DEEP, *hand colored, circa 1906.*

seems to jump out with three-dimensional ferocity and crudity. While no modern theatrical hand-tinting has been done, contemporary filmmakers such as Jules Dassin and Claude Lelouch have effectively adapted other antique effects such as occasionally tinting and toning sections of their films in much the same way as was common in the first two decades of the century.

Tinting (the immersion in a dye of the developed black-and-white film by which the entire stock is colored uniformly) can be seen in the amber-colored love scenes and blue-colored night driving scenes of Lelouch's A MAN AND A WOMAN (1966), while toning (chemical treating of the developed black-and-white image in which only the image is colored by altering the color of the silver deposit) survives in the brown-and-white images of the sepia night sequences of Dassin's 10:30 PM SUMMER (1966). Such current uses of the technique may impress modern audiences unaware that feature film prints in the collection dating from the twenties are likely to be on film stock tinted any of eleven standard colors. This process was used functionally—blue for night scenes—and often dramatically, as in the sudden plunging of the slightly tinted lavender into deep red in the Nazimova SALOME of 1922.

When the emulsion coating on the film was tinted one color and its clear celluloid base was toned another, a two-color effect was achieved, as in the combination of amber and green in the Goldwyn romance, A TALE OF TWO WORLDS (1922; fig. 2). The travel films and landscape shorts of the twenties attempted to use the tinting and toning effects to advantage as well, making the earth brown and the sky and water green.

In contrast to hand-coloring, and tinting and toning, "natural color cinematography" was attempted in 1909 with a process known as Kinemacolor. "Natural color" referred to the fact that Kinemacolor recorded directly on film from nature instead of applying colors artificially later. Its natural colors were virtually restricted to reds and browns, produced by the filming and projecting of its subjects through alternating filters while the frames on the film itself alternated between red and green. This effect presented to the eye, as the patent application worded it, "a satisfac-

Figure 3. Paul Ellis in THE GAUCHO. Kellycolor, 1927.

tory rendering of the subject in natural colors."

Kinemacolor—spotty, smeary, and suffering from a rash—was a successful vaudeville "act" reaching its greatest commercial standing with the longest film produced before 1911, the two and one-half hour newsreel of the crowning of George V as Emperor of India at the Delhi Durbar, its ceremonies and pageantry recorded by twenty-three cameramen.

An improved Kinemacolor known as Prizma appeared in 1916. One side of its film was coated red-orange, the other coated blue-green to give a compromise coloring to its subject matter. Prizma's OLD GLORY (1916) offers an accurate rendering of the United States flag, but gray skies and brown-gray grounds and buildings. A copy of Prizma's A DAY WITH JOHN BURROUGHS (1917) captures insects, flowers, children, and the eighty-year-old naturalist in primary reds and greens.

That same year the Technicolor Corporation produced THE GULF BETWEEN, a feature-length fic-

Figure 4. Erich von Stroheim in the two-color Technicolor portion of THE WEDDING MARCH, 1928.

The next year William van Doren Kelly, the developer of the Prizma process, introduced his subtractive process called Kellycolor. That Kellycolor was not as good as the perfected Prizma is shown by a 1927 two-reel drama in the process called THE GAUCHO (fig. 3).

Following the two-color Technicolor sequences in THE TEN COMMANDMENTS (1923) and BEN HUR (1925), it became the fashion to include color sequences in black-and-white films. Typically, color was not used to intensify dramatic development but to provide an interlude, as exemplified by the 1926 fashion show sequence of IRENE; by the Corpus Christi Day processional at St. Stephen's in Vienna with its plumes, epaulettes, and solemn cavalry in Stroheim's THE WEDDING MARCH (1928; fig. 4); and in thirty other films in a five-year period (1925-1930). Dramatically significant use of color would not appear until the last years of two-color Technicolor (1932-1933).

Mack Sennett, the pioneer comedy producer, introduced color in a subtractive red-and-green process he called Sennett Color into such 1928 two-reel comedies as THE SWIM PRINCESS and one that survives, THE CAMPUS VAMP (fig. 5), featuring Carole Lombard. Within the next year, over forty shorts were produced in two-color processes in America. This tremendous increase in volume resulted in quality control problems as well as the more basic problems inherent in any two-color process: a two-color process yields a compromise coloring with less pure values than are possible with three-color systems, which can theoretically produce any color in the spectrum. Two-color processes could reproduce pinks, salmons, browns, tans, red-orange, and blue-green but could not reproduce pure reds and yellows, neutral grays, light or deep blues, violets and purples.

Tony Gaudio, cinematographer of the first all-sound, two-color musical ON WITH THE SHOW (1929), remembered that certain colors were achieved by showing the camera an entirely different color, that "an unbelievable amount of light was needed," and that makeup was very unnatural.

Critics scoffed at "aluminum skies" and "revolutionary reds." Color became identified with the decoration of costume drama and formula musicals, as

tion film in Jacksonville, Florida. Its unsuspenseful and drawn-out scenario was designed solely to show off the colors best reproduced by the process. This was achieved by placing filters between the film and the screen during projection.

Although the principles underlying color photography were known as early as 1862, it would not be until the 1920s that a partially satisfactory color motion picture would be achieved. This came about as Technicolor dropped its additive color process (in which one color is added to another to produce a third color) and developed a subtractive process (in which colors are produced by filtering out other colors, each positive image being printed in a color complementary to the color of the filter). Technicolor's two-color process was used for Metro's TOLL OF THE SEA, a two-reel variation on "Madame Butterfly" with Anna May Wong, which was expanded into a full-length, five-reel feature and released in 1923. The film was praised for its bright, yet non-harsh colors and its "nearer simulation of nature." The film was a success, grossing $250,000.

typified by color sequences from THE DANCE OF LIFE (1929)—a Ziegfeld-like reel of production numbers—and from the remake of Mae Murray's PEACOCK ALLEY (1930).

Perhaps the best surviving example of the two-color Technicolor process is THE MYSTERY OF THE WAX MUSEUM (1933), the Warner Brothers film recently restored by the AFI in collaboration with The Museum of Modern Art. It·is still remarkable for the sharpness of its photography, its virtual absence of grain, and the rendition of its colors, but most especially for its use of a limited palette for effect: the lack of accuracy in its flesh tones was used to accentuate an eerie resemblance between the human actors and the museum's wax models, crucial to the effectiveness of the plot. In such sequences, dramatic mood was created by colored light and two-color renditions of the subject matter, so that no lack in the coloring was felt by audiences. But it came too late to restore faith in two-color films.

Within the year following the premiere of ON WITH THE SHOW, fifty-seven features used two-color Technicolor, thirty-four of them in release at the same time. Due again to problems of quality control in filming and printing, the results were often disappointing, both artistically—GOLDEN DAWN (1930)—and financially—KING OF JAZZ (1930).

By 1931, and the debut of red-and-green Multicolor, the boom was over. Multicolor would be used mainly in shorts such as the Universal series "Strange as It Seems," based ·on John Hix's newspaper feature documenting oddities of nature, an issue of which survives in the AFI Collection. By 1933, even the use of Multicolor in shorts disappeared, and it was through the use of the new three-color Technicolor in short subjects that interest was revived in color films.

The success of Disney's three-color Technicolor cartoons, FLOWERS AND TREES (1932), and THE THREE LITTLE PIGS (1933), not only prompted Columbia to produce its "Krazy Kat," "Scrappy," and "Barney Google" cartoons entirely in Technicolor by 1935, but also launched the first successful full-color system. From this time three-color Technicolor (fig. 6) would dominate until the introduction of Eastmancolor.

The film used to record the color information in

Figure 5. Sally Eilers in THE CAMPUS VAMP,
Sennett Color, 1928.

Figure 6. John Wayne and Chief Big Tree in SHE WORE A YELLOW RIBBON (1949), which won an Oscar for its three-color Technicolor cinematography.

three-color Technicolor was panchromatic silver bromide stock, each of the three black-and-white strips registering only the relative intensities of its primary color. In the special Technicolor camera, three black-and-white negatives, exposed at the same time behind their respective filters, combined to give a complete color record: a red barn in a green field photographed against a blue sky would leave on the red record negative an image of the barn; on the green record black-and-white negative an image of the field; and on the blue negative an image of the sky.

Each of the black-and-white strips yielded, upon printing, a positive relief image in which gradations were represented by varying thicknesses of hardened gelatin. This gelatin absorbed dye of the appropriate color. The dye images were transferred upon coated blank film, one after another, one for each primary color; and the resulting print became the projection copy sent to theatres.

Most color films of the time—with the exception of the self-conscious use of colored lights in the first live-action three-color Technicolor short, LA CUCA-RACHA (1934)—in attempting to avoid the charge of "postcard colors," copied 19th Century naturalistic painting in their exteriors, and the genteel, tasteful designs of home decorating magazines in their interiors. The results were unobtrusive, decorative, but rarely useful in intensifying dramatic effect.

Quite pleasing were the pastel blues and browns and soft skin tones of Magnacolor, a two-color process related to Prizma, Multicolor, and Kellycolor which was first used in Paramount's short subject series, "Popular Science" (1935-1939) and "Unusual Occupations," 1937-1939 (fig. 7), many of which are represented by original prints in the AFI Collection at the Library. Later, Magnacolor was used in full-length Westerns and melodramas produced by the subsidiary of Consolidated Labs, Republic Pictures.

Kodachrome—introduced in 1935—had five coatings of emulsion on one side of the film: three layers, each sensitive to its own primary color, and two layers for support. It was used primarily in 16mm non-theatrical productions for schools and industry, as in the 1943 U.S. Department of Agriculture film TREE IN A TEST TUBE (which includes the only color film appearance of the comedy team of Laurel and Hardy).

Figure 7. John Barrymore showing his stuffed animal collection in a Magnacolor episode from "Unusual Occupations," 1938.

A later variation called monopack—a single-strip color film—was used to record aerial footage for the Technicolor features DIVE BOMBER (1941) and CAPTAINS OF THE CLOUDS (1942), films which are among the sixty-five Technicolor features held in their original camera negative form in the AFI Collection. Although results with monopack did not equal those of the three-strip method for Technicolor release, it was the method by which World War II actuality footage in color would be seen in theatres, in such documentaries as WITH THE MARINES AT TA-RAWA, MEMPHIS BELLE, and BATTLE OF MID-WAY.

Gasparcolor, a three-color print process introduced in the mid-thirties, carried two light-sensitive layers on one side of the film and the third on the other side. Among the most notable examples of Gasparcolor in the Collection are George Pal's puppet animation advertising film SHIP OF THE ETHER (1934), produced for Philips Radio, and the beautiful abstract films of Oskar Fischinger, such as CIRCLES ("Kreise," fig. 8).

Cinecolor, yet another descendant of the Prizma process and perhaps the most successful of all, was first used for a feature film in 1942. In 1948, the combined footage printed by Cinecolor and Magnacolor

Figure 8. Oskar Fischinger's CIRCLES, Gasparcolor, 1933.

equaled the total Technicolor footage printed in the United States—more than 200 million feet of two-color film.

For the compromise color reproduction of two-color systems, makeup had to be light to avoid either sallow or red-orange flesh tones; sets and costumes had to be in pastel tones. Cinecolor and an improved version of Magnacolor were capable of producing pleasing skin tones and soft colors, despite an inaccurate tendency toward shades of green and orange. Representative examples in the AFI Collection include a dozen features from the studios of Columbia and Hal Roach, shorts from Warner Brothers and Paramount, including "Popeye" and "Looney Tunes" cartoons. The two-color films survived until the early fifties when Trucolor, a Cinecolor process, became three-color. But even with this improved Trucolor, best exemplified by Nicholas Ray's JOHNNY GUITAR (1954), Eastmancolor prevailed.

The most important breakthrough since the introduction of three-color Technicolor in the thirties came in 1949 with the debut of Eastmancolor negative and printing stock. Within five years the Technicolor camera was obsolete.

The end of the era of the Technicolor camera coincides with the discontinuation of the use of nitrate film base. Nitrate films are subject to deterioration within forty years of manufacture (a threat hanging over all films, black-and-white and color, on nitrate base, in use prior to the fifties); color films face further dangers, as exemplified by the original negatives for GONE WITH THE WIND: by the late sixties, the base of each of its three-color record negatives had shrunken, each to a different extent, so that it had become impossible to superimpose them in sharp registration by the use of the registration perforations on the films, some of which had been damaged.

Re-registration of the three color records had to be done by eye and required establishing a different relationship among the three positions than that given by the perforations. One color record was established arbitrarily as the standard, and the other two color records were conformed to it.

The color information contained in the black-and-white emulsions in the three-color Technicolor process is relatively stable because black-and-white emulsions are not subject to great change. In contrast, multiple-layer color films, such as Eastmancolor, are subject to some shifts in color and fading of the less stable dyes which provide the color.

Although dye stability has been improved in the last decade, processed film which is to be kept for a long time (for archival purposes or for anticipated re-issue) has to be given attention so that color shifts can be minimized. This is done by careful washing at the time of processing, controlling temperature and humidity at the place of storage, and periodic inspection of the color films.

The best method of guaranteeing permanence of the color image is by making black-and-white records, one for each of the primary colors. This doesn't make a color image immediately available for inspection but a color negative and a print for screening can quickly be made from this negative. It is an expensive method, not only because of the initial preparation of the three separate records, but also for the later reconstitution of the color image, with the subsequent requirements of retiming within a decade's time.

In the past three-quarters of a century, patent offices have recorded dozens and dozens of ways of effecting color motion pictures. Every possible method —and many an impossible one—has had its moment and then disappeared. Of the few systems that were successful, most are obsolete, their achievements remaining in the two-color and three-color examples which survive.

No color movie process is capable of reproducing every color in the spectrum with complete accuracy at the same time: there is only an indirect relationship between the colors of the subject as perceived by the eye and colors available through dyes. But this is not to deny the effectiveness of Technicolor or Gasparcolor or of the many two-color processes in those films which are their finest achievements. The secret of eloquent color in movies may well lie elsewhere than in an obsession with literal color accuracy.

Tom Shales

THE MYSTERY OF THE WAX MUSEUM

Warner Brothers. 1933.
Director: Michael Curtiz.
Screenplay: Don Mullaly and Carl Erickson,
based on the play by Charles S. Belden.
Cast: Lionel Atwill, Fay Wray, Glenda Farrell, Frank McHugh.

Fay Wray as the wax figure of Marie Antoinette in THE MYSTERY OF THE WAX MUSEUM.

It is one thing to recall the technical processes that have come and gone and another to see them in action. THE MYSTERY OF THE WAX MUSEUM was one of the last films to be made in two-color Technicolor, an interim stage between tinted films and three-color Technicolor. WAX MUSEUM demonstrates how a limitation was kept from becoming a handicap—the film does not suffer under the restriction but, in fact, benefits from it. Directors in later years would try for some of the same effects even though three-color Technicolor had long since been taken for granted.

"You fiend! You fiend!" cries Fay Wray, as Lionel Atwill clutches at her with his gnarled hands. She has just shattered his false face with her fists and revealed the hideous, charred distortion beneath. He prepares to tie her down so that hot wax can be poured over her naked body, encasing her for eternity.

Thus comes the climax of the early thirties horror classic THE MYSTERY OF THE WAX MUSEUM, directed by Michael Curtiz in 1933 and long thought to be, in the words of horror scholar Carlos Clarens, "irretrievably lost."

What makes the film significant? First, its excellence and artfulness, both relatively rare to the genre. Second, the fact that it was shot in the two-color Technicolor process. That, in fact, was a prime reason for the film's apparent disappearance. WAX MUSEUM was one of the last features to be made in that process, and its replacement by advanced color technology eventually made it impossible to print negatives from the original two-color version. The color version was never shown on television and never reissued, and was thought lost until a print turned up in the private collection of Jack L. Warner. That print was copied onto modern color negative stock (THE MYSTERY OF THE WAX MUSEUM was preserved in color through a joint effort of The Museum of Modern Art and The American Film Institute), and the film has thus been restored to public view.

The two-color Technicolor adds the ideal eerie glow to the story of dark doings in London and New York of the twenties and thirties. While flesh tones registered faithfully, technicians were unable to achieve true greens, true yellows, and other colors. The resulting blue-green, reddish-orange aura added to the film's creepiness, as it did to an earlier and similar film, DR. X (1932), also shot by Ray Rennahan (WAX MUSEUM's photographer), directed by Curtiz, and featuring many of the same cast.

Ironically, WAX MUSEUM is less familiar to today's audience than is the generally inferior remake, HOUSE OF WAX, directed by Andre de Toth and released by Warners in 1953. (Roger Corman also used the basic story for one of his own variations, A BUCKET OF BLOOD, in 1959.) In one dramatic respect, HOUSE OF WAX has an advantage: the 3-D process, refined for the film's 1971 reissue. It also benefits from the score by David Buttolph. Though his music is not exceptional, at least it's there. WAX MUSEUM has only three bursts of music: the opening credits, the fade-out, and a scene in which an on-screen radio is chirping out "A Shanty in Old Shanty Town." Then, too, the 1933 script was littered with loose ends of plot and needless people, all streamlined out of the fifties' slicker rewrite.

But what it may lack in these miscellaneous sophistications, WAX MUSEUM makes up for in lurid details and characterization, the latter best represented by Atwill's demented artist (a character not dissimilar to the scarred composer of THE PHANTOM OF THE OPERA), leering at his wax creatures and acclaiming "the texture of that flesh" in gruesome tones, and by Glenda Farrell, as the hot-shottiest of tough girl reporters.

Many films of the period relied on newspaper characters to advance the plot briskly and maintain a steady upbeat of snappy pseudo-journalese. Miss Farrell's girl reporter is a classic example. She marches smartly into police headquarters and greets a cop with, "Hi, sweetheart, how's yer sex life?" She argues furiously with her editor (Frank McHugh), warns him at one point, "If you wisecrack while I'm talking, I'll crown ya," and dismisses another potential opponent with, "Okay, brother, then you can go to some nice warm place and I don't mean California." When faced with fright, she mourns, "Oh, what I wouldn't give for a slug'a'gin," and when, at the end of the film, the editor finally asks for her hand (and the rest of her) in marriage, she snaps, "I'm gonna get even with you, ya dirty stiff! I'll do it!"

Lionel Atwill in THE MYSTERY OF THE WAX MUSEUM.

WAX MUSEUM's most telling details, though, are its horrific ones—the fire at the beginning, with the lifelike figures melting into grisly oozes; nighttime in the city morgue, with a dead body suddenly popping up as a side effect of embalming fluid; one of Atwill's workers lovingly sliding a dagger into the body of Marat as the New York wax museum readies for its opening; chases through shadows as the ghoulish sculptor collects bodies for his exhibit; and, of course, the shock when Atwill's homemade wax face crumbles to the floor and exposes the hidden demon.

Part of the film's suspense, too, derives from the wax figures themselves. We can't be blamed for wondering which are really fakes and which are actually live actors holding their breaths. If you watch closely, however, during a scene in which Atwill conducts a tour of his museum, you may be able to see Queen Victoria blink.

Matthew Betz, Lionel Atwill, and Allen Vincent in
THE MYSTERY OF THE WAX MUSEUM.

The destruction by fire of Lionel Atwill's life work in THE MYSTERY OF THE WAX MUSEUM.

Michael Curtiz

Tom Santschi in THE THIRD DEGREE, 1927.

Hollywood has always been a melting pot, and in the twenties and thirties, one of the primary ingredients was Germanic. Directors and other craftsmen from Germany and Austria were attracted to what was then the movie capital. The immigrants included such luminaries as Stroheim, Lang, Lubitsch, Murnau, Veidt—and Michael Curtiz, who would prove to be one of the most versatile of the group, and also exhibit remarkable staying power. Curtiz directed everything from melodrama to musical to swashbuckler to thriller. He was at home with them all.

By 1926, the year Michael Curtiz arrived in America, he was already an established director in the European cinema with over sixty feature films to his credit. Working for a variety of studios in Hungary, Denmark, Germany, France, and Austria, he had gained a reputation for producing films with striking visuals, dramatic staging, and sweeping action; but very few of these efforts have survived. Therefore, until the discovery of Curtiz's first American film, THE THIRD DEGREE (1927), by The American Film Institute, it was nearly impossible to gauge the extent to which his mature style had developed during the silent period.

In this respect THE THIRD DEGREE is a genuine revelation, for it is literally a showcase of the major characteristics that form the Curtiz style. Clearly, he was making every effort to impress his new audience and his new employers. As Curtiz later admitted, he realized that his entire career depended upon how strongly he could depict this rather tired story of a rich man's son being disinherited for marrying beneath his social class. Never again would Curtiz so blatantly reveal his directorial hand as in the film's flamboyant, expressionistic sequences and tricky subjective shots; at one point the camera even plays the role of a lethal bullet.

Curtiz's oft-noted expertise at staging exciting action is evident throughout THE THIRD DEGREE, but most spectacularly in the precisely edited opening scene, a circus stunt aptly titled "The Whirl of Death." His penchant for camera movement is demonstrated by numerous crane-shots (he and cameraman

NOAH'S ARK, 1929.

Errol Flynn in THE ADVENTURES OF ROBIN HOOD, 1938.

Hal Mohr had to construct their own boom out of a telephone pole), dolly-shots of varying speeds and functions, and sinuously twisting tracking shots. Curtiz's seemingly intuitive visual sense, recognized by Mohr, is evident in the tasteful, if sometimes extreme, angles; the space-defining foreground object compositions; and the luminescent close-ups. Certain shots, including three superimposed views of the protagonist climbing endless stairs, a huge close-up of a grossly distorted ear, and a multiple view of an old woman's jabbering mouth, suggest the influence of THE LAST LAUGH and VARIETY. In the film's most powerful and unusual scene, a "third degree" in which the police force the innocent hero to confess to a murder, Curtiz uses his entire expressionistic vocabulary to compel the audience to experience the victim's hysteria.

THE THIRD DEGREE apparently had the desired impact, at least as far as Curtiz's career was concerned. The validity of his techniques was debated in various newspapers, denied in *The New Republic*, and affirmed in *The New York Times*. But, more important, the film sufficiently impressed the Warner brothers. They offered Curtiz a new long-term contract with a considerably higher salary than had originally been agreed upon.

Of the nine films that followed, only one, the two-million-dollar NOAH'S ARK, is known to exist at this writing. Unfortunately, the only print generally available is a drastically re-edited and cut-down version that was marketed for church groups in the mid-fifties. Even that print, however, is conclusive proof of Curtiz's ability to create stunning spectacle with great visual style.

With the exception of MAMMY (1930), a lively minstrel drama starring Al Jolson, Curtiz's first sound films reveal only too clearly the inherent limitations of the new medium. Curtiz had been struggling with these difficulties since TENDERLOIN (1928), the first film with an extended dialogue sequence, and on THE GAMBLERS (1929) he had been the first to restore the camera's mobility by mounting the soundproof "ice box" on wheels. Still, many of his films of the period, such as THE MATRIMONIAL BED (1930) and GOD'S GIFT TO WOMEN (1931), were static and talk-dominated.

CAPTAIN BLOOD, 1935.

Michael Curtiz on location for the charge sequence from
THE CHARGE OF THE LIGHT BRIGADE, 1936.

Sydney Greenstreet and Joan Crawford in FLAMINGO
ROAD, 1949.

Curtiz returned to form with THE MAD GENIUS (1931), a consistently intriguing account of a megalomaniacal Russian dance impresario (obviously modeled on Diaghilev). It was the first of Curtiz's films to deal in an extended manner with the theme of cynicism versus idealism which he would return to repeatedly throughout the rest of his career.

From this point on, Curtiz's films of the early thirties show an increasingly assured approach. THE WOMAN FROM MONTE CARLO (1932) is the first in which he made characteristic use of camera movement to force the tempo of intrinsically static dialogue sequences. THE STRANGE LOVE OF MOLLY LOUVAINE (1932), which reveals Curtiz's desire to force the pace still further with fast, overlapping dialogue, is also notable for a continued emphasis on the question of moral attitudes, a more subtle sense of character, and a far grittier *mise-en-scène*.

Curtiz's involvement with films of social relevance began with CABIN IN THE COTTON (1932). It placed Richard Barthelmess in the dilemma of having to choose between corrupt Southern landowners, represented by a surprisingly provocative Bette Davis, and exploited but vicious tenant farmers. Other punchy Curtiz message pictures followed, including 20,000 YEARS IN SING SING (1933), BLACK FURY (1935), and MOUNTAIN JUSTICE (1937).

Of the three horror-type (Warners never ventured into pure horror) films directed by Curtiz, the most interesting and inventive is THE MYSTERY OF THE WAX MUSEUM (1933), another recent discovery of the AFI working in collaboration with The Museum of Modern Art. Besides being the only available example of Curtiz's use of the two-color Technicolor process, THE MYSTERY OF THE WAX MUSEUM perfectly demonstrates his ability to sustain a mood of suspense and foreboding in a contemporary setting.

Although Curtiz was never associated with the popular string of Warners gangster films during these years, he did pioneer in the genre that was to replace it: the detective film. His THE KEYHOLE (1933), PRIVATE DETECTIVE 62 (1933), THE KENNEL MURDER CASE (1933), and THE CASE OF THE CURIOUS BRIDE (1935), stylishly depicted different types of the new screen hero from the urbane Philo

Vance to the witty and absolutely cynical Perry Mason (lawyers, like newspaper reporters, now became little more than detective surrogates).

While Curtiz's best films are usually concerned with a protagonist who is racked by some inner conflict, the series of adventure films he made with Errol Flynn featured a more aggressively self-confident hero. Here the central theme became one of the individual's defiance of society as represented by figures of authority. In CAPTAIN BLOOD (1935), Flynn rails against the English king and various judges and governors; in THE CHARGE OF THE LIGHT BRIGADE (1936), he is a British Army officer, forced into insubordination when he can no longer accept the bungling of his superior officers; in THE ADVENTURES OF ROBIN HOOD (1938), he is, of course, the archetypal rebel of all time; and in THE SEA HAWK (1940), he expresses his by-now-expected impudence toward both Queen Elizabeth and numerous representatives of the Spanish government. These films gave Curtiz full opportunity to exhibit his mastery of atmosphere and violent action (fencing duels became succeedingly more elaborate) and their financial success allowed him to assume the unchallenged position of Warners' "ace" director.

Sandwiched in between the rousing swashbucklers and genteel comedies of the late thirties were two realistic melodramas that typified Warners' concern with the urban milieu. KID GALAHAD (1937) anticipated by a decade the "gloves-off" look at boxing in post-war films like BODY AND SOUL (1947) and THE SET-UP (1949). In KID GALAHAD, Curtiz detailed the sordid aspects of the fight scene, the raucous hotel parties, the gambling and gangsterism, with the same care he lavished on the brutal fight scenes. Equally hardboiled was ANGELS WITH DIRTY FACES (1938), with James Cagney in one of his best roles as the anarchic Irish gangster Rocky Sullivan.

ANGELS WITH DIRTY FACES stressed the relationship between crime and the deprived urban environment, emphasizing the detrimental example of Cagney's successful gangster career on the kids in his tenement neighborhood. However questionable the morality of the ending, with Cagney feigning coward-ice to deter the "Dead End Kids" from a life of crime, ANGELS WITH DIRTY FACES remains one of the most exciting and polished films from this phase of Curtiz's career.

During the forties, as his powers continued to develop, his position as one of Warners' top directors enabled him to display his versatility by producing masterpieces in a variety of genres. THE SEA WOLF (1941), with its violence (sixteen fights and two suicides) and ideological confrontations, was ideally suited to Curtiz's skills. An excellent script by Robert Rossen, a fine cast headed by Edward G. Robinson, and an ominous Nietzchean score by Erich Wolfgang Korngold made this film the definitive cinema adaptation of Jack London's adventure classic.

Switching with apparent ease from a film of unrelieved fatalism to one of unabashed optimism, Curtiz in 1942 directed YANKEE DOODLE DANDY, possibly the finest musical biography ever filmed. James Cagney is magnificent as George M. Cohan, and Curtiz keeps the action moving at breakneck speed. The exuberance of this flag-waving extravaganza fulfilled the patriotic needs of the wartime era, though the film also served a historical function by nostalgically chronicling the turn-of-the-century vaudeville milieu.

In 1943 Curtiz finally received national recognition with an Academy Award for CASABLANCA (1942), not only his best-loved, but also one of his most typical films. The conflict between cynicism and commitment was perfectly expressed by Bogart, with the rest of the Warners stock company neatly embodying a wide range of moral attitudes.

In 1943 Curtiz directed MISSION TO MOSCOW, a large-scale Stalinist apologia made at the request of President Roosevelt (according to Jack Warner) to aid in the "understanding" of our Russian allies. It clearly demonstrates Curtiz's ability to make even the most intransigent and unpromising material move on the screen.

At the end of the war years, Curtiz returned to his specialty, the realistic melodrama, with his 1945 version of James M. Cain's *Mildred Pierce*. Curtiz, scriptwriter Ranald MacDougall, and Joan Crawford humanized Mildred's character somewhat, but the film,

like Cain's novel, paints a bleak picture of southern California, with its tract housing, drive-in restaurants, and decaying Spanish-style mansions. Curtiz's absolute mastery of dramatic visuals is nowhere better illustrated than in this naturalistic saga of American grass-widowhood.

In 1946 Curtiz was invited to join Liberty Pictures, a sort of directors' cooperative formed by Frank Capra, George Stevens, and William Wyler. Fearful of losing Curtiz, Jack Warner gave him an "autonomous" unit within the studio. Michael Curtiz Productions began operations in 1947 with an ambitious list of projects including James M. Cain's *Serenade*. Unfortunately, Warners still had financial control over the new company, in addition to final approval on all scripts. After the studio had rejected several screenplays, Curtiz quickly produced and directed THE UNSUSPECTED (1947) to fulfill contract obligations. The result was a somewhat confused but highly entertaining *film noir* centered around a diabolical Alexander Woollcott-like radio commentator played with great relish by Claude Rains. In spite of its high style, THE UNSUSPECTED was a box office disappointment. Curtiz's discovery of Doris Day precipitated a series of generally vapid musicals designed to get the new company out of the red. His last independent production was FLAMINGO ROAD (1949), a rambling story of political corruption marked by beautiful high-contrast photography by Ted McCord and excellent performances by Joan Crawford, Zachary Scott, and Sydney Greenstreet.

In 1949, tired of responsibility without freedom, Curtiz sold his company back to Warner Brothers and returned to the studio he had never really left. His later films are, of course, after the nitrate era, but the Curtiz films in the AFI Collection should do much to bring recognition to one of the most neglected directors in the American cinema.

Edward G. Robinson in THE SEA WOLF, 1941.

Sol Polito, Michael Curtiz, Olivia de Havilland, and Errol Flynn on the set of THE CHARGE OF THE LIGHT
BRIGADE, *1936.*

David Thaxton

MISSION TO MOSCOW

Warner Brothers. 1943.
Director: Michael Curtiz.
Screenplay: Howard Koch, based on the book by Joseph E. Davies.
Cast: Walter Huston, Ann Harding, Oscar Homolka, George Tobias, Gene Lockhart, Eleanor Parker.

Walter Huston meets Stalin (Manart Kippen) in MISSION TO MOSCOW.

One of the most interesting things about MISSION TO MOSCOW is that it was made at all. Preserving it means granting access not just to another political era but to another sensibility—a different stage of the ever-changing national consciousness. Through the attitudes that went into its making, we can feel and appreciate sentiments of another time.

One of the most unusual and controversial pictures in The American Film Institute Collection is MISSION TO MOSCOW, directed by Michael Curtiz, produced by Warner Brothers, and released in the spring of 1943.

When the movie was released, *New York Times* critic Bosley Crowther wrote that it was "clearly the most outspoken picture on a political subject that an American studio has ever made." Based on the best seller by Joseph E. Davies, Ambassador to the Soviet Union from 1936 to 1938, MISSION TO MOSCOW, the peculiar product of Hollywood's wartime enthusiasm, argued persuasively that Americans should be more concerned with winning Russia as an ally in the fight against international fascism than with irrational fears about communism. As Walter Huston (playing Ambassador Davies) explained it: "How they keep their house is none of our business. I'm concerned with what kind of neighbor they'll be in case of a fire."

Implying that European reactionaries had caused the war, MISSION TO MOSCOW ridiculed the position held by American isolationists and characterized Stalin as kindly and benevolent "Uncle Joe." In its zeal to depict the Soviet Union in a favorable light, MISSION TO MOSCOW even attempted to justify the 1937 purge trials, the Nazi-Soviet Non-Aggression Pact, and the Russian occupation of Finland. Suggesting that there really was no difference between the United States and the Soviet Union, MISSION TO MOSCOW was, as James Agee put it, "a great glad two-million-dollar bowl of canned borscht, eminently approvable by the Institute of Good Housekeeping."

MISSION TO MOSCOW may not have seemed very radical to Americans in sympathy with the "One World" politics of Wendell Willkie or Henry Wallace,

Ann Harding, Eleanor Parker, and Walter Huston watch a German youth group parade in MISSION TO MOSCOW.

A frame from a World War II "war effort" appeal trailer.

but it was quite a departure from Hollywood's past treatment of the Soviet Union. Moreover, it had been only a decade since Roosevelt had established diplomatic relations with the Russian government, and the ideology of international liberalism was far from universally accepted. Walter Huston, who also narrated the "Why We Fight" series for the United States Army, was a perfect choice for the film's progressive ambassador, for he brought to the screen the same dignity and authority which he had established with previous roles in films like ABRAHAM LINCOLN (1930), AMERICAN MADNESS (1932), and DODS-WORTH (1936). And the use of newsreel footage and documentary techniques made the picture even more persuasive. Supported by Max Steiner's score and the brilliant camerawork of Bert Glennon, the film was impressive wartime propaganda.

Though shown extensively in the United States and Russia during the war, MISSION TO MOSCOW proved an embarrassment after 1945 to everyone involved in its production and was quickly withdrawn from distribution. In 1947, the House Un-American Activities Committee called on Jack Warner, then head of production at the studio, to explain why MISSION TO MOSCOW had been made. In the studio's defense, Warner stated that "if making MISSION TO MOS-COW in 1942 was a subversive activity then American Liberty ships which carried food and guns to Russian allies and the American naval vessels which convoyed them were likewise engaged in subversive activities. The picture was made only to help a desperate war effort and not for posterity." Anxious to determine if the White House had pressured Warner Brothers into making the picture as a "patriotic duty," HUAC continued to probe, but Jack Warner's answers were vague. He was more specific, however, in his denunciation of writers in the Warners' stable whom he fired for being "Communist propagandists." Among these was Howard Koch, author of the screenplay for MISSION TO MOSCOW. Though Koch was not blacklisted with the "Hollywood Ten," he found it hard to find work during the next decade.

For most of the post-war period, it was difficult, if not impossible, to see MISSION TO MOSCOW. In the sixties, however, the film began to appear once again in film study programs and on television. And its preservation insures that future generations of students and scholars will have access to one of the strangest documents of our political and cultural history.

Thomas Ince

David Shepard

Thomas H. Ince did everything. He was so proficient at every aspect of filmmaking that even films he didn't direct have the Ince-print, because he exercised such tight control over his scripts and edited so mercilessly that he could delegate direction to others and still get what he wanted. Much of what Ince contributed to the American film took place off the screen; he established production conventions that persisted for years and, though his career in films lasted only fourteen years, his influence far outlived him.

Such is the longevity of scandal that most people who know of Thomas Ince at all remember his death, under what are vaguely described as "mysterious circumstances," aboard the yacht of William Randolph Hearst. Ince's death was due to natural causes, and there is no particular mystery about it. Is it then more appropriate to remember Ince as the man who organized film production in the pattern which was known for two generations as the "studio system"? Despite the reports of standard film histories, J. Stuart Blackton had established the "studio system" years earlier at Vitagraph. What about Thomas H. Ince, the great director of THE COWARD, THE NARROW TRAIL, THE BATTLE OF GETTYSBURG, and CIVILIZATION? Ince directed precious few of the films that appeared under his name, and none at all after 1915; he edited and approved scripts, edited and approved pictures, and left the actual writing and direction to frequently anonymous associates.

And yet, in *The History of Motion Pictures*, Bardeche and Brasillach concluded, "Ince was infinitely superior either to Griffith or to Cecil B. De Mille." They report that Louis Dulluc compared Ince to Rodin, to Debussy and Dumas, even to Aeschylus. "He is the first," Dulluc wrote, "to synthesize the confused but brilliant impulses of this art as it emerges from the matrix." Jean Cocteau, writing about one of Ince's epic films in 1916, said that "a spectacle such as this seems in recollection to equal the world's greatest literature." In his lifetime, Ince was called "the enigma of picture drama." Today there are shelves of books on filmmakers from Griffith to Godard, but the only book on Ince is his autobiography—

William S. Hart, the good-badman and one of Thomas Ince's best known stars.

stored in manuscript at New York's Museum of Modern Art, forbidden to researchers, and unknown even to Ince's grandchildren. Forty-eight years after his death, Ince is still an enigma.

My own first attempt to penetrate the mystery aborted in 1963, when I stepped to a phone, gulped twice, and called C. Gardner Sullivan for an interview. Sullivan had been Ince's most constant and capable writer-director for almost the entire length of Ince's film career. "God, no," he said. "If people knew I'd directed William S. Hart, they'd think I was five hundred and four."

Still, it must have been quite a time. Ince's first films in California were made on 14,000 acres of land leased from the Santa Monica Power and Light Company in the then-empty area between Beverly Hills and the Pacific coast. A tribe of Sioux roamed there, brought by Ince to the Pacific coast and allowed to live free in return for war-paint appearances in the magnificent Westerns from which Ince's reputation has justly endured. Inceville, his first studio, was a ramshackle affair situated where Sunset Boulevard meets the sea, but when Ince was there, no roads reached it; Alice Terry remembers being met each day at the end of the streetcar line by a stagecoach in which the company rode to work. By 1916, Ince had an agreement with Harry Culver for a free studio site on the real estate Culver developed as the city which bears his name; today, it is MGM. His last studio was right down the street—and the lovely neo-classic administration building which doubled as a set in BARBARA FRIETCHIE and many other Ince pictures remained famous as the trademark of one of its subsequent occupants, David O. Selznick, who used its likeness together with a motto: "In a tradition of quality."

Ince was certainly a mystery worth unraveling. Fortunately, material on his films, though scattered, was not unknown. George Pratt, who has done the most extensive and responsible research on Ince, had collected many scripts, still photographs, interviews, and films for George Eastman House in Rochester, New York; scrapbooks, stills, and a few other films were donated by Mrs. Ince to The Museum of Modern Art. In Paris, the Cinémathèque Francaise has still

more film, together with the fine John E. Allen Collection of Ince scripts and memorabilia. The Library of Congress had a few Ince films among the paper prints, restored to view during the sixties. AFI acquired some Ince films from individual private collectors.

Our first inkling that an untouched cache of Ince material might still exist came in 1965, when a man known to UCLA as "a Mr. Gladden of Encino" gave the University some two dozen 16mm prints of Ince features produced between 1916 and 1924. I spent Christmas holiday in Los Angeles and screened the prints. They were in mint condition, and obviously made from original negatives. Did the negatives exist? They did indeed, and Mr. Gladden produced nitrate material on fifty-five silent features. In January of 1969, AFI began to negotiate with UCLA for acquisition of the Ince films, and between that time and December of 1971, when the films finally reached our hands, we little by little learned the details of a fascinating story that reveals a great deal about the casual and almost accidental way so much of the primary source material of film history was conserved.

After Ince's death in 1924, the production of pictures immediately ceased, although the company remained active for the administration of real estate and other holdings. Many of the old negatives were junked right away. Others were sold. CIVILIZATION, Ince's epic answer to Griffith's INTOLERANCE, went for $750 in 1929. 23½ HOURS LEAVE, Ince's most famous comedy and the film which established director Henry King, was sold to its star, Douglas MacLean, for $1,000 in 1932. Other negatives decomposed, and the remaining films were about to be discarded from storage in the garage of their custodian, former Ince associate Roy Purdon, when he mentioned their existence to his friend Tholen Gladden. Gladden arranged to stash the negatives in unused vaults at his employer's studio—the same vaults originally built by Ince, for Gladden worked for RKO which had by now acquired Selznick's lot.

Gladden edited George Stevens' I REMEMBER MAMA during the day, and working nights and weekends, he wound through the Ince film. He discovered that the negatives were completely out of sequence, for scenes had been arranged for printing by color

Thomas H. Ince and President Woodrow Wilson.

tints rather than by story progression. Some of the eighty or ninety small rolls which made up each feature had been lost; other tinting rolls had decayed; but by sagacious trimming and patching, a large group of films were reconstituted and printed up for a new and hungry market—television.

Alas, nothing could then have seemed less interesting or more irrelevant than these films. Who in 1950 would be entertained by DANGEROUS HOURS, a 1919 melodrama of the *first* "Red scare" with characters like Boris Blotchi, the lurid Bolshevik; suffragette Sophia Guerni; or idealistic student John King? The *second* Red scare with characters like Senator Joseph McCarthy made better drama. The films failed to arouse any interest, so Purdon and Gladden, together with Thomas Ince, Jr., and attorney Sanford Carter, gradually accepted the loss of the money they had spent to reprint the films and the waste of work it had taken to trace and clear the rights on all of them.

UCLA now agreed it did not have funds or facilities to assure the permanent preservation of the films, and Mr. Gladden agreed with Mr. Carter that the material was of cultural and historic interest and that it belonged in an archive. Final word, however, could be given by only one person—Mrs. Thomas H. Ince (Elinor Kershaw), who had worked nights with her husband, helping to edit his films and build his empire. In her eighties, she lived quietly in Palos Verdes, away from the movie colony.

Early one morning, Kevin Brownlow, his wife Virginia, and I went to visit Thomas H. Ince, Jr., recently widowed, who lived alone in a modest house in San Pedro. Ince ushered us into his living room, decorated with trophies of auto and speedboat victories. When he saw that our interest was genuine, he brought out pictures of Inceville and memories of his own achievement, interrupted by a nearly-fatal accident in 1942. We talked about Ince scripts, for we had seen a big box of them the week before during a visit to the stored remains of the failed Hollywood Museum. "I donated those," he said. "You see, I needed a filing cabinet, and rather than buy a new one, I just emptied an old one of its contents and gave them to the museum."

We were incredulous. "You mean you had a whole filing cabinet full of stuff like that?"

"There are *thirty-six* filing cabinets full," he said, "in our old office up on Franklin." He then described a building which his father had owned and mostly rented, except for one office in which the old company records remained in storage.

"See Mr. Burke. He's there on Thursdays," Tom said. "He'll show them to you."

Tom promised to talk with his mother in our behalf. As we left, he said to us, "You know, I was only twelve years old when my father died. Think what I might have become if he had lived." The three of us crossed the street and took a long, quiet walk on the beach.

A few Thursdays later, we called the number Tom had given us for Mr. Burke, which we discovered to be wrong. We called Tom back to confirm the number and couldn't reach him. A few weeks later he was dead.

"I talked to my grandmother, and she wants to see you." Now I was visiting Tom's daughter, Nancy Ince Probert. A charming, down-to-earth woman, she raised horses and ran an airline with her husband Dick. Nancy described her grandmother as "kinda conservative, so be on best behavior." I cut my hair in preparation for a luncheon date on Friday, but age and illness again intervened, and it was finally Nancy, who had never seen an Ince film, who called Mr. Burke.

The building on Franklin had not been painted for many, many years. At the bottom of the stairs there was a sign: "Thomas H. Ince Corporation," and at the top, an old office, designed to satisfy in 1920 and since left unchanged. George Washington looked down from the wall; the oil painting had been a prop in an Ince film.

"Mr. Ince liked that," said Mr. Burke. "He had that on the wall when he was here."

"Did you work for Mr. Ince when the company was making pictures?"

"I was with him for a while, but left before he died. I came back later. I was the head of the payroll department." Vigorous, scrubbed pink and with close-cropped white hair, Mr. Burke was obviously older than he looked. He left us on our own to go to work, and we began to pull open one file drawer after another.

We had learned by then to recognize the thrill of the hunter before the kill, of the philosopher at the instant of insight, of the archaeologist as the tomb lid lifts. It came to us at that moment.

First we found contracts, Ince's agreements with his stars, including Charles Ray, Dorothy Dalton, William S. Hart, and Enid Bennett. His agreements with his writers were there. His tax records, back to 1913. The corporate seal and corporate minute books. Hundreds of scripts, all the drafts of them, and directors' copies marked with shooting order and changes made during production. Distribution agreements and other business papers made it clear that Ince had reduced the making and distribution of pictures to a science by 1918. Each Hart, Ray, Dalton, and Bennett film came in within two or three thousand dollars of its projected budget—and each earned within five or six thousand dollars of its projected worldwide income. Taking into account such diversified markets as Denmark, Japan, and Brazil, Ince could gauge the distribution and earnings of his product as exactly as if he were making bicycles or shoes.

The Ince business papers and films, now in the AFI Collection, await serious study by researchers. A commercial distributor has licensed rights to the films from Nancy Ince Probert, Tholen Gladden, and Sanford Carter, and as the pictures reappear, perhaps new interest will emerge and some of the mysteries still surrounding Ince and his work may start to unravel.

The Ince papers and films are being supplemented by other historical research. King Vidor has given his oral history to interviewer Nancy Dowd; Henry King has talked to Tom Stempel; Rowland V. Lee has written a splendid autobiography. All were once Ince directors. These projects were conducted by the AFI with support from the Louis B. Mayer Foundation.

This is the data from which the history of film will someday be rewoven. It largely remains to be sifted, and in that project, a great challenge awaits.

The Ince company at Inceville, 1912-1913.

William K. Everson # The "B" Western

Frank Jennings (left) and Al Jennings (right) in
THE LADY OF THE DUG-OUT, 1918.

Harry Carey in John Ford's STRAIGHT SHOOTING, 1917.

We might view the "B" Western as one huge movie, its individual scenes not of themselves exemplary, perhaps, but the total picture a pop artifact that also embodies many of the most telling trademarks of the American film. Fast, vital, efficient, succinct, with characterization quickly developed and resolution swiftly sought, the "B" Western reflects not only our film values but our Judaeo-Christian, pioneer-spirit, actions-speak-louder-than-words American values as well. "B" Westerns concern a heritage, but they have become a heritage themselves.

Perhaps before talking blithely about the status and importance of the "B" Western, we should establish what it really is. The term "B movie" has always been tossed about casually and contemptuously, implying economy of budget and paucity of talent. Yet everything is relative: the MGM "B" would be the Allied Artists "A"; and film history has shown, too, that the box office "B" of yesterday can prove to be the artistic "A" of today.

In the case of the Western, however, the boundaries are more clearly defined. Although there is a tendency for the general public to tar all "B" Westerns by the same brush and accept the lowest common denominator of quality as being the average, there is an enormous range and variety in the content of style of the "B" Western. "B" in this case denotes neither quality nor cost but merely an exhibition classification: films made to a set pattern, usually six to eight a year, each studio featuring a given star or stars in series which all have their own format and almost identical running times (the "B" Western as described here virtually disappeared in the mid-fifties).

Even within these limits, however, there were no rigid rules. Some of the Hopalong Cassidy Westerns ran close to ninety minutes, as did the elaborate Roy Rogers musical Westerns of the forties. Such films were second features in large cities and major top-of-the-bill attractions in rural communities. Production costs were far from standardized. Ultra-cheap quickie Westerns, devoid of such niceties as the use of camera trucks or musical scores, or the luxuries of retakes when scenes misfired, were sometimes brought in for as little as $3,000—including the salary of the star! Other "B" Westerns, made by major studios such as RKO—with more facilities, a reputation to protect, and of course better exhibition outlets—often reached budgets of $90,000. When one six-reel Western can cost thirty times as much as another, it must be apparent that there are wide divergencies in quality!

It should be remembered that the "B" Western quite probably offered more artistic freedom to the director than any other kind of film. This is not to say that many directors took advantage of it, nor that the hundreds of "B" Westerns lying in studio vaults contain scores of unappreciated masterpieces. But the director of the "B" Western, working away from the studio, his product not important enough to warrant supervision or interference during or after production, was literally free to do as he liked. As long as he brought in a saleable product on time and on budget, nobody cared whether he made a poetic masterpiece or five reels of fisticuffs.

Many of our finest directors—John Ford, William Wyler, William K. Howard, W. S. Van Dyke, Edward Dmytryk— came from, and learned their trade in, the "B" Western. And the care and love for their craft *show* in their earlier Western efforts. A former editor like Joseph H. Lewis, assigned to direct a handful of the Johnny Mack Brown Westerns for Universal in the forties, demonstrated how a little extra effort and affection could bring real style to the most commonplace of plots. His ARIZONA CYCLONE is full of sequences carefully broken down into well-composed shots; focus changes within a shoot-out confrontation to heighten tension; and chase scenes brilliantly strengthened by unusual compositions and camera devices to give an even greater illusion of speed. I doubt if all this care brought in an extra dime at the box office, but it showed that Lewis understood and loved the art of making movies. His above-average Westerns proved to be valuable stepping stones to much more important things.

The expertise of the stuntwork in the Republic Westerns of the thirties and early forties, done by Yakima Canutt and his team long before they became recognized for their work in BEN HUR and similar prestige films, is a model of speed, efficiency, and

Harry Carey.

breathless excitement that many a bigger film could have benefitted from.

The stunning camerawork of a man like Frank B. Good is another of the artistic bonuses of many "B" Westerns. A look at his WHEN A MAN'S A MAN (an exceptionally good George O'Brien "B" of 1935) shows that the camerawork can hold its own with the work of Bert Glennon in a John Ford super-Western. And the stars themselves, deserving of course far more space than these few lines, were often far from "B" in quality. Admittedly, the poverty-row quickies boasted a few stars who were helpless off a horse, and who couldn't get through a single line without fluffing, but at the other end of the scale one has the incredible showmanship and trick-riding expertise of Tom Mix and Ken Maynard, the genuine acting ability of a Buck Jones, and the breezy geniality and sense of humor of a George O'Brien.

Vast masses of audiences know the myth of the West (somewhat inadequately, it is admitted) and the art of the Hollywood Western almost entirely through the "B" Western. Gene Autry undoubtedly made a greater impact on larger audiences than the documentary austerity of such classic spectacle Westerns as Walsh's THE BIG TRAIL or Vidor's BILLY THE KID. Such a large body of popular and influential movie-making deserves to be taken seriously, preserved, and studied; and it's good to find that The American Film Institute's extensive Western collection includes—in bulk—representative examples of the best, the most typical, and probably (by mass acquisition, rather than intent) the worst of the "B" Westerns.

Students of the genre may well be surprised at the adult stature of the scripting and the creative photographic style of such early Columbia talkies as Buck Jones' THE AVENGER, or even more, the sincerity and dedication to the espousing of the Indians' cause in Tim McCoy's END OF THE TRAIL, a pocket (and poetic) BROKEN ARROW. The same studio's END OF THE TRAIL with Jack Holt will also surprise (or shock) those who insist on perpetuating the myth that the Western plot is just a collection of cliches. How many big, deluxe, prestige Westerns of today would have the guts to finish up with the hero going to the gallows for the killing of the villain?

Through the AFI's Western collection, one can also study the quite astonishingly superior production values of RKO's George O'Brien Westerns or, at the other end of the scale, marvel at the production ingenuities that enabled Warners, by cunning scripting and careful matching up, to build most of their John Wayne Westerns of the early thirties around spectacular chunks of footage from First National's silent Ken Maynard films—and then to use footage and plots all over again for a third series of Westerns with Dick Foran.

If researchers are thus inclined to categorize Warners Western movie-producers as ragpickers, hopefully they will then be directed back to some of the *original* silent Ken Maynard vehicles, in particular THE RED RAIDERS. Not only is it unsurpassed as a showcase for Maynard's extraordinary riding skill and sociologically interesting for its approach to Indian problems, but it is perhaps an extreme example of the fantastic excitement and huge-scale action typical of the silent Western devoted almost exclusively to thrills. THE RED RAIDERS may lack the poetry or inspiration of STAGECOACH, but it is visualized on an even grander scale, and its Indian attack scenes are still some of the finest ever put on film.

Among other Westerns in the AFI Collection is STRAIGHT SHOOTING, John Ford's first feature and a film in which many of the roots of his later classics can be seen. Also included is THE LADY OF THE DUG-OUT, starring Al Jennings, who was a direct link with the Old West in that he was a bandit (of no noted efficiency) who was pardoned and took up the movies, allegedly reconstructing his life on film but actually conforming very rigidly to the good-badman image of William S. Hart, and presenting his life strictly in "B"-movie terms. But then we'd probably all be happier if our lives ran as smoothly and as predictably as most—but not all—"B"-movie scenarios.

Ken Maynard and Ann Drew in THE RED RAIDERS, *1927.*

Tom Shales

THE VANISHING AMERICAN

Famous Players-Lasky. 1925.
Director: George B. Seitz.
Screenplay: Ethel Doherty, based on the novel by Zane Grey.
Adaptation: Lucien Hubbard.
Cast: Richard Dix, Lois Wilson, Noah Beery,
Malcolm McGregor, Nocki.

Richard Dix in THE VANISHING AMERICAN.

It's easy to see only the forest when some of the trees are missing. Fortunately, many can be found again. Now in the AFI archives is the only known complete 35mm print of a 1925 film that defied stereotype, questioned tradition, and told a palpable story as well: THE VANISHING AMERICAN. Until it was acquired with a group of other Paramount silents, it seemed to have vanished, too. The film deserves to be known. And now, it has been made possible that it will be.

American Indians have not, as a rule, been treated fairly, even decently, in sound films. In thirties Westerns, they were usually portrayed as savage and uncivilized scalphunters. Silent movies of the twenties, however, tended to give Indians a bit more respectability. Of these, THE VANISHING AMERICAN (1925) is one of the best and most beautiful.

George B. Seitz had an unspectacular directorial career (including the 1922-1923 serial "Plunder," with Pearl White) until THE VANISHING AMERICAN. Instead of depicting him as a wanton savage, the screenplay by Ethel Doherty, from a Zane Grey novel, tried to invest the Indian with a tragic stature and correct the myths about his warrior impulses.

The attempt seems noble in retrospect, though the film, viewed through contemporary eyes, looks just as racist as a lot of other pictures from the past. Its theory that one race replaces another, that each progressive race is superior to the last, seems a trifle fascist besides. But in its time, THE VANISHING AMERICAN was no respecter of the usual cliches.

In addition, it has a rather awesome sense of history as a pageant played out across vast vistas—the vistas strikingly photographed by C. Edgar Schoenbaum and Harry Perry. Titles refer to "the mighty stage," a setting that will remain after all the races kill one another off. Looking at life in grand terms like this was typical of the silent epic, but the film has a humanity and credibility that make it seem somehow more honest and immediate than many films of its era.

THE VANISHING AMERICAN begins with an elaborate prologue in which one race dissolves into

52

Richard Dix and Lois Wilson in THE VANISHING AMERICAN.

Richard Dix and Lois Wilson in THE VANISHING AMERICAN.

the next—from cavemen to basket makers to the cliff dwellers, who herd turkeys and wash in mud. And then, from "no man knows whence," cometh the Indian, "terrible and swift as a pestilence," we are told. In one of the film's most effective outbreaks of spectacle, the Indians sweep down a river valley, overwhelming the cliff dwellers in a semi-poetically filmed battle. Before it ends, a cliff dwelling priest will intone a curse: "May Paya the Father drive you into darkness, as you drive us! May he send a stronger race to grind you into the dust and scatter you through the four worlds of lamentation." You'll never guess who that stronger race turns out to be.

In the film's view, the Indian is truly mistreated, but that is just the nature of things, the law of civilization, the relentless onward trudge of mankind. THE VANISHING AMERICAN was ahead of its time, but it was no LITTLE BIG MAN. In the 1925 film, the Indian is most laudable when he is most convincingly mimicking the white man—reading the Bible or joining the U.S. Army to help fight World War I. The villainy perpetrated against him, we may thus infer, is despicable only because the Indian was trying to be as good as white folks are and wasn't given enough

of a chance. Compared to the attitudes expressed in other films, however, this was progress.

Richard Dix plays the Indian Nophaie with dignity and credibility, even when the script calls for him to submit in deferential piety to the wonders of the New Testament. When he returns from the war to find his people cruelly cheated by unscrupulous whites, he goes out to pray to his gods. This, he decides, will get him nowhere; his religion is "foolish," and he casts it aside, relying instead on the Bible given him by white woman Marion Warner (Lois Wilson). Finally, when he dies (even though the Bible in his pocket has partially deflected the fatal bullet), he asks that the Scriptures be read to him and, expiring, gasps, "I . . . think . . . I understand." This is apparently to assure us that he has earned a ticket to white man's heaven—his redemption is due to his acceptance of the dogma of a "superior" race.

Sociological limitations seem minimal, however, when compared to the physical luster and narrative power of the film. THE VANISHING AMERICAN has not vanished; it remains—compassionate and impassioned cinema.

Kathleen Karr

Early Animation: The Movement Begins

Pvt. Mutt and Miss AWOL confront Judge Gloom on a speeding charge in AWOL, circa 1918.

Pvt. Mutt in the brig in AWOL, circa 1918.

From GERTIE THE TRAINED DINOSAUR to FRITZ THE CAT—a long way and, in another sense, one small step. No history of animation can be written without reference to the name of Walt Disney, but there were many other pioneers, perfecters, and practitioners of the animator's art. Often, ideas developed by independent artists found their way to the mouse factory, but the give-and-take was productively mutual, if not always voluntary. Animation goes back to the beginnings of film itself, and the movement continues.

Animated cartoons are the indirect result of 19th Century experimentation with optical toys. Panoramas, dioramas, and zoetropes all gave the illusion of movement to drawn landscapes or figures, foreshadowing the more successful illusions of motion pictures. While scientists and inventors were experimenting with optical toys, quick-sketch artists of the vaudeville circuits were amusing audiences with their manual dexterity and wit, and newspaper cartoonists were establishing a market for their delightful cartoon characters. As with most technological innovations, then, it was a convergence of many elements which permitted and supported the production of animated cartoons.

There were two requirements. Because of the method of animation production (the need for many individual drawings, each slightly different from the one preceding it), speed and dexterity were of the essence for the animation artist. There was also the necessity of a narrative line which would please an audience, and for this the newspaper cartoonist was well prepared.

After the early novelties of watching pure motion in drawing, the audience wanted more to keep its attention. Thus, American animated cartoons expanded from the charming but basically non-story meanderings of Winsor McKay's GERTIE THE TRAINED DINO-SAUR to the whimsical social commentaries of the Hearst-Vitagraph "Phables" (little stories involving the exploits into the human world of dozens of "Joys" and "Glooms," stick-like characters who perform the function of a chorus commenting on the foibles of men). There were, of course, natural transitions from newspaper cartoons to movie cartoons, which were aided by newspaper syndicate financing for promo-

Rodolph Vaselino finds true love on the screen in Walt Disney's PUSS IN BOOTS, *1922.*

Puss comes to the aid of her master.

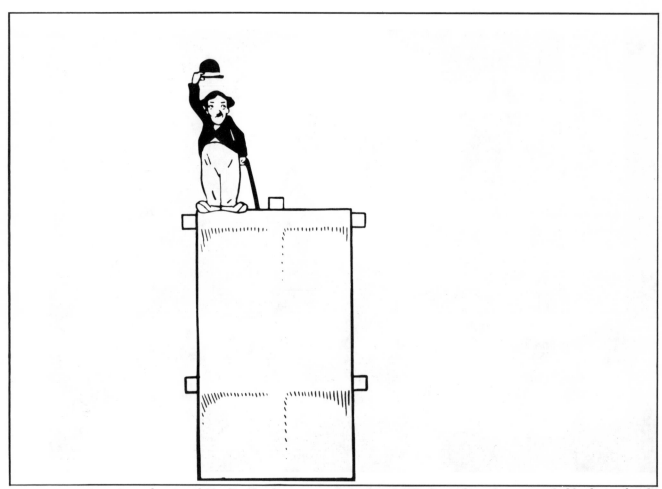

An animated series of Charlie Chaplin cartoons helped to fulfill the audience's unquenchable desire for the little tramp in 1916. This is a scene from CHARLIE AND THE WINDMILL.

The opening title of an early twenties "sing along" cartoon.

tional purposes: George Herriman's "Krazy Kat," Bud Fisher's "Mutt and Jeff," and Pat Sullivan's "Felix the Cat" soon found their way into the movies. Most of these split-reel films were audience successes. Surprisingly little of this pre-sound era animation exists today, but what little of it does remain proves strongly the form's popularity, inventiveness, and ability to teach as well as amuse.

One of animation's strong points was its ability to parody the world of humans. Walt Disney's "Silly Symphonies" of the early- and mid-thirties relied heavily on this aspect of the genre. Among Disney's most striking examples are his caricatures of movie stars in MICKEY'S GALA PREMIERE and WHO KILLED COCK ROBIN. In his 1922 PUSS IN BOOTS (the second major cartoon of his Kansas City period and considered to be lost until recently added to The American Film Institute Collection), we find Disney caricaturing Rudolph Valentino in BLOOD AND SAND (and stealing a bit of that picture's plot as well). Another aspect of this ability to parody is the series of split-reel Charlie Chaplin cartoons made in 1916 by the Herald Film Corporation. The Collection's only example of this series, tentatively titled CHARLIE AND THE WINDMILL, also exploits the figures of Fatty Arbuckle and Mabel Normand trying to dislodge Charlie from his perch atop a windmill with carefully aimed bricks.

Animation's ability to educate in very broad and easily acceptable terms was demonstrated by the War Department's commissioning and use of animated cartoons for training U.S. troops during World War I. The Fox Film Corporation, which distributed the Bowers Studio's "Mutt and Jeff" series, was commissioned to make at least seven known titles for this purpose. Among them were HUNTING THE U-BOATS, JOINING THE TANKS, and LANDING A SPY. Unfortunately, only one of these Bowers war films seems to have survived—AWOL ("All Wrong Old Laddiebuck")—an apparent post-war effort designed to keep the troops on their foreign bases till Uncle Sam could ship them home. A "Mutt"-like army private is tempted off-base by a gorgeous "Miss Awol," in a little roadster named "Joy." The private's joy ride ends in his return to base and his imprison-

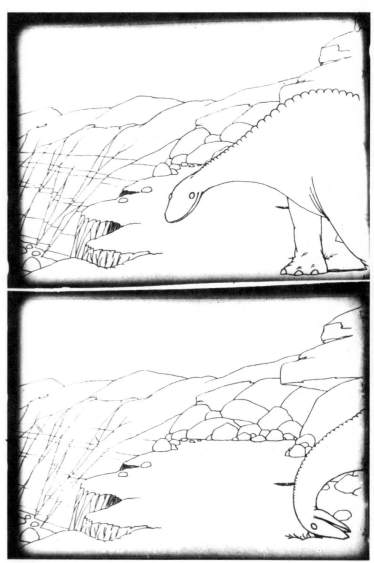

Winsor McKay's GERTIE THE TRAINED DINOSAUR, 1914.

ment for being AWOL while all the other enlisted men cheerfully skip back to America.

Later animated films in the Collection include a series of "Popular Song Parodies," short program fillers derived from the old song slide presentations in which a bouncing ball dances over the lyrics of popular songs (presumably to keep the audience and piano player in tempo), followed by little stories which satirize the songs. Also included is THE SNOW-MAN, a Cinecolor fantasy by Ted Eshbaugh, one of Disney's competitors in the early thirties song-and-color cartoon craze, as well as a wonderful collection of the experimental animation of Oskar Fischinger. Fischinger, a German-born artist who spent his later life in the United States, was interested in the play between form and color (one could compare his filmed experiments with those of Joseph Albers in paint, although Fischinger's work is less rigid); and his films, along with the work of light theorist Thomas Wilfred, strongly influenced much of Walt Disney's FANTASIA.

Animation holds an important place in any overview of film history. Through its experimental phases, it is a popularization of modern art; through its caricatures and ability to educate it throws light on popular American culture, decade by decade. Animation can be as subtle or as flagrant as any live-action feature film, and it can achieve these effects in mere minutes before an audience.

The Black Film Experience

Stephen F. Zito

Old films sometimes remind us of things we might like to forget. Black films of the past, viewed from the vantage point of today, reveal some of the foundations for racism and intolerance that still persist and still cause shock waves and remorse through society. But in addition to the ill treatment of blacks in films made for white audiences, there was also a long-ignored genre of films made for black audiences (often by white directors), sometimes mere translations of established white genres, and sometimes starring such widely known black stars as Dizzy Gillespie and Cab Calloway.

Rosetta Duncan (in blackface) as Topsy in
TOPSY AND EVA, 1927.

The image of the black man in the American film has changed radically in recent years. The invisible man has become visible, and all the good grey Toms and shiftless Rastuses of yesteryear have quit stealing chickens and are out making it with white women and cutting up Mafia hit men. A first generation of black superstars has been born and is playing out a new collective role—that of the Negro as street fighter and hustler, a high-style achiever who overcomes a hostile world by means of street cunning and a strong arm. The recent films that create this image (notably SHAFT, COTTON COMES TO HARLEM, and SWEET SWEETBACK'S BAADASSSSS SONG) also represent the first viable organization and expression of ghetto experience in American films. The city cat has taken the place of the country mouse, and this black cat (partly a fantasy projection and partly a closely observed, realistic type) is a character of multiple and shifting human dimensions.

The recent films dealing with black experience take on a special meaning when they are viewed within the context of the past history of the Negro in films. The Negro traditionally had but three roles to play: the savage, the fool, and the castrated Uncle. And the Negro actor playing these roles has less inhabited them than been bound and gagged by them. Black character has been dictated by popular stereotypes, and these stereotypes have been created out of a very few histrionic elements: the shuffled step; the molasses-slow, stumble-tongued patterns of speech; the razor in the torn pocket; and the watermelon grin. As

SPYIN' THE SPY, 1917.

Stanley Cavell wrote in *The World Viewed*, "Until recently, types of black human beings were not created in film. . . . We were not given, nor were we in a position to be given, individualities that projected particular ways of inhabiting a social role; we recognized only the role." The Negro actor has not only been forced to work within certain circumscribed roles and certain prescribed gestures, but he has also, at times, been reduced to providing humor merely by being black.

The American Film Institute has preserved three silent comedies that, taken together, not only indicate the unsettling, unsympathetic portrayal of the Negro in early American cinema but also show to what extent the blackness of the black man was both his badge of character and his comic fate. One of the earliest of these films is SPYIN' THE SPY (1917), a racist comedy in which the black hero becomes involved with an imitation Ku Klux Klan group. Another is ANDY'S LION TALE (1925), a two-reel comedy directed by Francis Corby that was one of a series released by Universal between 1923 and 1928. The film was based on "The Gumps," a syndicated newspaper comic strip written and drawn by Sidney Smith. "The Gumps" featured a "typical American family" and was known for poking gentle fun at the foibles of the chinless Andy Gump and his household. ANDY'S LION TALE has little feeling for the characters and situations of the comic strip and is, instead, a slapstick comedy in the tradition of Sennett and Roach.

In the film, an escaped lion gets loose in the Gump household and terrorizes everyone in sight, including three Negro servants, who all register exaggerated fright with the rolled eyeball and the blubber lip. The dialogue titles as well as the overt action of the film are blatantly racist: one of the servants appears to dissolve in fright, his remains being left behind in the form of a pile of coal dust; the Negro cook remarks, "Them lions crave dark meat"; two of the black men hide beneath the covers of a bed, and when the lion finds them and licks their feet, their faces turn white in fear; a pair of trick eyeballs as large as grapefruits makes one of the Negroes appear to be a hysterical hypothalamic. What is remarkable about ANDY'S LION TALE is not that the film perpetuates both the

The Miller Brothers and Lois in HI-DE-HO, *1947.*

Lucia Lynn Moses in THE SCAR OF SHAME, 1927.

usual Negro roles (cooks and servants) and the accepted Negro characteristics (childish, easily frightened, cowardly, stupid) but that the film's prime source of humor is the *color* of the black men and not their characters at all. The gags cited above all have their origin in color: black men turn white, break down into coal dust, and are really only dark meat. The humor is literally skin deep and reduces Negro selfhood to the matter of color.

Another film that deals with this comedy of complexion is HIS DARKER SELF (1925), a farce starring Lloyd Hamilton as a white writer of detective fiction who disguises himself as a Negro in order to clear his Negro servant of murder charges falsely leveled against him. The film presents Negro life and character within the narrow limits of the black man as a being of frantic passions, primitive angers, and sudden violence. The sequences of the movie that are set in Darktown take place in public places like a dance hall and a river baptismal (Negroes presumably not having homes or families), and when the brute black men are not drinking and whoring, they are playing dangerous games with knives. HIS DARKER SELF was originally intended as a vehicle for Al Jolson, the greatest of the blackface performers, but the role was given by default to Lloyd Hamilton when Jolson became camera-shy and went to Europe. Hamilton's career was primarily as an actor in short comedies, and his impersonation of the Negro character is broad and superficial. Although he is supposed to be playing a dual role, Hamilton merely blackens his face with burnt cork and plays the same character in both black and white. HIS DARKER SELF is a film with one joke—a white man pretends to be a black man—and its humor is largely reductive: all personality and all community life are boiled down to a single equation: to be black is to be inferior is to be funny.

The most extreme and racist of the silent comedies preserved by the AFI is TOPSY AND EVA (1927). The film is based on a stage play of the same name by Catherine Chisholm Cushing that was in continuous performance on the American stage between December 30, 1923, and May 9, 1925. The play was based on some of the characters and events in Harriet Beecher Stowe's *Uncle Tom's Cabin* (and on a subsequent dramatization of the novel), but many incidents were added, eliminated, or rearranged. The film essentially takes the relationship between Topsy, "the black imp," and Eva, "the white saint," and makes these two children the focal interest of what had once been the tragic story of a man called Tom. Uncle Tom does, at least, appear in a marginal role in the film and is played with quiet dignity by Noble Johnson. This dignity does not, however, compensate in any way for the manner in which Topsy is played by Rosetta Duncan, a white performer who began her career in 1916 as a yodeller on a vaudeville stage in San Francisco.

Topsy is one of the most damning examples of racist portraiture in the American film: she is ignorant, thieving, superstitious, undisciplined, uneducated, and given over to swearing and biting; she eats bugs picked from flowers and butts heads with a goat. And she is repeatedly characterized as dirty. After she is sold at auction for five cents to Little Eva, Topsy is given her first bath; she fights against the water, and a dog, after sniffing in disgust at her old clothes, takes them out and buries them. The dirt, however, seems to be more symbolic than real, for dirt is somehow equated with being black. Topsy prays to God to change her color ("I won't ask you to make me white as Eva—just a nice light tan will do"), and the color of her skin is understood to be the cause of her badness of character. TOPSY AND EVA has elements of Christian parable: Topsy, the bad child, is bad because she is black; she becomes good by following the example of Little Eva, the good white child. The film is about a black character redeemed by becoming white in all things except color. And color is one thing that will never wash away.

The history of the Negro in the American film is more extensive and varied than has been, until recently, either known or cared about. The traditional narrow roles and racist themes in Hollywood films have been a matter of record and common knowledge. There were some films made outside of Hollywood, however—films in which Negro life and character were presented in a favorable and even heroic light. These films were made with all-black casts and were intended for showing in the almost 500 movie houses that were "for colored only." The films were made quickly and cheaply by independent companies (occasionally operated with black capital), and they are not much in the way of art. They are, however, generally entertaining and full of the myths and surfaces of several generations of black Americans.

The first company producing all-black features for the ethnic market was the Lincoln Motion Picture Company, founded by George P. Johnson around 1916. The company managed to stay in existence for several years and seems to have made at least five films, several of which starred George Johnson's brother, Noble. These films have disappeared, but the AFI has acquired and preserved a silent black feature, THE SCAR OF SHAME, which was produced by the Colored Players Film Corporation of Philadelphia in 1927. The actors in the film were black; the producer, Sherman H. Dudley, was a Negro comedian who worked primarily in vaudeville. The director of the film, Frank Perugini, was a white journeyman director who learned his trade while working as a photographer on independent Westerns like THE VALLEY OF LOST SOULS (1923); and the cinematographer on THE SCAR OF SHAME was Al Ligouri, a freelance cameraman who sometimes worked at the Paramount studio on Long Island. The fact that the technical crew on the film was white is yet another indication that training for black technicians was virtually unattainable until recent years. And it was just this lack of skilled black labor that goes a long way toward explaining why there is only a very short history of any kind of viable, widely exhibited ethnic cinema in this country.

THE SCAR OF SHAME is a carbon copy of a genre (society melodrama) that was turned out by the gross in the Hollywood studios of the twenties. What gives the film its great interest is that the story has been filled out and translated into the terms of Negro life. The film was partly shot on location in the Philadelphia suburbs, but more interesting than its rare glimpses of middle class Negro life are the fantasies and longings expressed in the film. The plot features adultery, rape, murder, and a prison break, but the film is really not about these things at all. Rather it is a study in caste and class and color among black people who are torn between their passions and the

65

KILLER DILLER, 1948.

desire to be respectable. As is so often the case in black films, the "good people" in the story are light-skinned and the "bad people" are dark-complected. This color-keying is a form of visible shorthand, a means of immediately identifying those with whom the audience is supposed to be in sympathy.

The story revolves around an uneducated, dark-skinned girl who forces an upright, middle-class piano teacher into marriage. The film ends with the suicide of the woman, and nowhere is one kind of black self-destructiveness more clearly traced to the longing for a whiteness that can never be achieved. THE SCAR OF SHAME expresses in the most poignant manner the needs of the black woman to find acceptance and status in a milieu where class is a matter of color as much as a matter of money or education.

THE SCAR OF SHAME is one of a very few silent black films known to exist; there are, fortunately, a number of sound films that have survived. These films are not of very high cinematic quality, but the best of them are good enough, and all of them are of interest. The decline in quality from the high standard of a film like THE SCAR OF SHAME can be directly traced to economic factors. The companies financing the black features worked with minimal capitalization and sold their product in a limited, static market. The increased cost of sound recording had to be met by cutting back on other aspects of production; and the films suffered because of these enforced economies. TEN MINUTES TO LIVE, for example, a gangster film made by Oscar Micheaux of Harlem, is not nearly as polished or professional a film as THE SCAR OF SHAME. Not only did the quality of black films change with the coming of sound, but their very nature changed as well.

Several of the silent all-black features were honest attempts to deal with such controversial topics as race prejudice and passing for white. The sound films, in contrast, are less interesting thematically, being roughly divided into two groups: canned vaudeville and variety acts, like JIVIN' THE BE-BOP (Dizzy Gillespie), HI-DE-HO (Cab Calloway), and JUNCTION 88 (Pigmeat Markham); and routine imitations of standard Hollywood genres—gangster films, newspaper films, murder mysteries, even romantic comedies, like GIRL IN ROOM 20 and KILLER DILLER (with Butterfly McQueen of GONE WITH THE WIND fame).

A representative sampling of the sound films made for ethnic audiences would include a trio of films dealing (ostensibly) with life in Harlem: MYSTERY IN SWING, MOON OVER HARLEM, and MIRACLE IN HARLEM. The titles are promising, seeming to indicate an authentic thirties view of Dark Manhattan. The films, however, do not live up to the promise of their titles.

MOON OVER HARLEM (1937) is the best of the lot, but it does not transcend its gangster genre so much as work adequately within it. The film, directed by Edgar G. Ulmer, was made in the same year that Ulmer directed THE SINGING BLACKSMITH, a film in Yiddish that was released in this country with English subtitles. The Yiddish market existed alongside the Negro market, and someday it would be instructive to compare the films made for their very different audiences.

Ulmer was an ex-patriate Viennese who started out as an art director for Max Reinhardt in the theatre, later designed sets for F. W. Murnau, and finally turned to directing. His career is more obscure and peripheral than most, but he is a minor cult figure, having once been praised by Andrew Sarris as a director who, faithful to the Murnau trust and having his own visual style and signature, was "one of the minor glories of the cinema."

MOON OVER HARLEM shows little sign of either style or signature. It is, instead, a straightforward melodrama about white and black gangsters in Harlem. The central black gangster is a worthless man who marries a woman for her money, tries to seduce the woman's teenage daughter, and is killed when he goes up against a Mafia extortion team. The nominal hero of the film is a community organizer who attempts to band Harlem merchants together in an effort to put an end to the extortion racket. He neither succeeds nor fails at this task, but one of the merchants he talks to says to him, "I like the way you talk. It makes us all seem more like men." The film is realistic in its depiction of underworld activities and offers a collective solution to urban crime that

Butterfly McQueen in KILLER DILLER, 1948.

is more hopeful than helpful.

Like many films made for black audiences, MOON OVER HARLEM is, in many ways, both conventional and conformist. Ulmer insists on the fact of Negro achievement; for example, showing the ingenue as upwardly mobile—she goes to college and plays girls basketball. The organizer is in love with the ingenue, and their courtship is extremely proper and discreet. The film also has a little edge to it. There is some street talk and bravado, and a naked girl in a bathtub. There are also some jokes about color. In one wry exchange, a woman remarks, "When I get married, you know, I'm gonna marry me a real high yella. He may beat me but I know my good home cooking will bring him around." MOON OVER HARLEM reflects the caste and color consciousness of a previous generation, to some of whom being black meant being Negro and being light meant being a little bit less Negro. It was made at a time when many bars in Harlem would not serve dark-skinned Negroes, and serves as a reminder, if we need one, that to the Negro himself, black was not always beautiful.

MYSTERY IN SWING (1940), on the other hand, is a straight newspaper comedy-melodrama that features a wisecracking reporter who solves a murder with the help of a girl reporter and an irascible editor. The film is structured like a traditional murder mystery: one murder, several suspects, and enough suspicious circumstances to make everyone appear to be guilty. The film was written by Arthur Hoerl in a manner both competent and perfunctory, and directed by Arthur Dreifuss, a German who alternated between directing dance sequences on "A" pictures and making short subjects at Columbia. The direction by Dreifuss is smooth and uninspired, reminding one that the film looks like a sepia-toned version of a Columbia "B" picture.

The third film in this "Harlem Trilogy" is MIRACLE IN HARLEM (1948), one of the few ethnic pictures to be reviewed in the trade press. It was praised in *Film Daily* as a "shrewd blending of drama, religious overtones, crime, romance, music and comedy." The film was directed by Jack Kemp, a former editor on all-black features, and its plot has to do with a murder in a candy store. The romantic leads in the film (handsome, enterprising, achieving) are played by Sheila Guyse and Ken Freeman who, at that time, were appearing nightly in Kurt Weill's "Lost in the Stars" on Broadway and making MIRACLE IN HARLEM during the day. The comic relief in the film is provided by Stepin Fetchit, who, having been squeezed out of Hollywood for his offensive portrayals of the black man, kept right on doing his same shuffling, lazy routines in films made for all-black audiences.

The sound films about life in Harlem lack documentary verisimilitude. They are not records of how life was actually lived—of real people or places or things. They are, instead, as fantastic and contrived as the Hollywood product of the period. While watching them, however, there is a shock of recognition as one realizes that, for once, black actors have all the lines and are playing heroic and romantic black characters who do not roll their eyeballs or tote razors or take large, grinning bites of watermelon.

The real meaning of the black films is ultimately to be found in their intentions. The films may sometimes be crude and even laughable, but only because they are not well made. Their importance is that, at a time when white audiences thought the role played by Stepin Fetchit was a realistic interpretation of Negro character, there were films that attempted to represent (not misrepresent) all kinds and degrees of Negro character—good and bad, and all the shades in between.

THE EMPEROR JONES

Tom Shales

United Artists. 1933.
Director: Dudley Murphy.
Screenplay: DuBose Heyward, based on the play by Eugene O'Neill.
Cast: Paul Robeson, Dudley Digges, Frank Wilson, Fredi Washington, Ruby Elzy.

Paul Robeson confronts the jungle in THE EMPEROR JONES.

The play's not always the thing—sometimes it's the players. A principal value of many films lies in the permanent recording of a great performance—John McCormack in SONG O' MY HEART, or Helen Morgan in the De Forest Phonofilm excerpt from the original "Show Boat." For power and bravado though, there are few filmed performances of the era to match Paul Robeson's in THE EMPEROR JONES. Now preserved from a reassembled print, it remains as strong and stirring as it was when Robeson first did it, on the stage of the twenties and the screen of the thirties.

It took months of painstaking work to track down and then piece together existing prints of THE EMPEROR JONES, but it was worth it, not so much for the film itself as for its lead performance—the very definition of a tour de force by a great actor, Paul Robeson.

All existing 35mm prints and negatives of the film appeared to have been destroyed, so The American Film Institute sought out whatever 16mm materials could be found. Those that were uncovered were all incomplete, but together they made up, in bits and pieces, a complete print of the film. After the print was patched together, a new sound track was made, as well as a new negative from the 16mm reconstruction. Thus has the film been restored to the public eye.

Whatever the strengths of the screenplay by DuBose Heyward (author of "Porgy")—the first portion of the film is new material written by Heyward—they are diminished in comparison to Robeson's powerful performance. It is a role the singer-actor had already played to perfection on the stage. It is difficult to ascribe credit for the direction of the film because William de Mille took over sometime during the production for Dudley Murphy. But whatever the virtues of the direction, the greater glory is undeniably Robeson's.

Naturally, Eugene O'Neill's play seems light-years from racial enlightenment now. The blacks in the film are predominantly shiftless shoe-shiners, fulfilling many of the most egregious but established stereotypes of the period. But Robeson's performance in this film is a proud and emphatic one—even when saddled with a line like "Feet, do your duty."

The Edward Steichen portrait of Paul Robeson as The Emperor Jones.

The revival meeting in THE EMPEROR JONES.

O'Neill's story is a fable about a lowly man's rise to power. The theme that power corrupts is diluted by the fact that Brutus Jones is depicted as rather corrupt from the beginning. Few valid conclusions can truly be drawn from it—except perhaps that man is a creature who ought to fear himself more than anything else—although the fable structure keeps seeming to be portentous or rich with message.

But Brutus Jones becomes an unforgettable character in Robeson's hands, from the opening shot, when we catch him admiring his new brass buttons in a mirror, the device he loves so dearly. This scene is intercut with a revival meeting at the Hezekiah Baptist Church in honor of Jones' departure for a life of promise. Only at the end of the scene, when Jones enters the church, do we learn what his great fortune is—he has become a Pullman porter. Smiling, Robeson leads the congregation in a hymn. He sings three spirituals in the film with his own special strength: "Water Boy," "Now Let Me Fly," and "I'm Travelin'."

"Trouble's my buddy," Jones will declare later, and the friendship soon begins. He is callously untrue to his trusting girlfriend-back-home and even alienates the affections of his pal's gal. In a sultry bedroom scene, he decides to desert her too because, he says, the longer one keeps a woman, the harder it is to "tote" her. "Here's forty dollars and good-bye," he says, and the scene shifts to a smoky, shadowy honky tonk, where a young kid tapdances in tails and the opening moans of "St. Louis Blues" are sung by a trio. There Brutus will accidentally stab his pal Jeff (Frank Wilson) after a crap game. Brutus runs, the saloon returns to normal, with the body lying seemingly unnoticed until a cop appears. Then, cut to marching feet, chained together, legs in prison stripes, we hear Robeson's plaintive "Water Boy" and know what has happened.

He kills a guard and escapes, then jumps a boat off the island of Haiti, where the pre-Papa Doc dictator wears a top hat and masterminds a profitable economy. Eventually, Jones will overthrow him by pretending to be a god—a native shoots him, and he doesn't die because he has secretly filled the gun with blanks.

Brutus Jones admires his mirror image.

73

"I's charmed!" he shouts defiantly. "It takes a silver bullet to kill Brutus Jones!" He becomes the ruler, redecorating the palace, literally, in his own image: "And then I wants mirrors—plenty of 'em!" He mulls over the possible titles to befit himself. Mr. President? King Brutus? Those don't "make enough noise." Then comes the moment of self-proclamation: "The Emperor Jones!" he bellows, and the world really does seem to shudder in the wake of it.

It may sound as if the role is all bravado, but Robeson gives it subtlety and passion that are enormously moving, especially in the last two reels of the film when, with doom approaching and beating drumlike in the distance, the Emperor is reduced to the lowly man who is at the core of emperors everywhere. He runs into the jungle carrying a revolver loaded with one silver and five lead bullets. Haunted by ghosts of the past, pursued by his own fears, even abandoned by his god, he is humbled and defeated, resorting finally to a desperate crawl. Before the end, he takes the silver bullet from its cylinder and holds it up to the light. "Don't she shine pretty?" he says,

envisioning the peace that awaits him in the heavenly kingdom promised by the preacher at the Hezekiah Baptist Church.

At this climax, the film achieves a universality. The racial stereotypes can be forgotten, the occasional archness of the fable ignored. Jones has gone down, but Robeson has conquered the limitations of the play, the character, and the film. He has made it something finer than what it was, and this incomparable performance is now, once again, intact. Ironically, although Brutus Jones has proven less than an exemplary emperor—he has embodied the worst of all possible rulers—we are not encouraged by his collapse. He made a point, earlier, that helps explain why; "There's big stealin' and little stealin'," he said, and for big stealin' "they makes you Emperor and puts you in the Hall of Fame when you croak." That most of the big stealers escape Jones' fate may be one of the still relevant themes of the play and film. Its dominant element, however, for all those who have seen him in the role, will always be Paul Robeson.

The Movies Learn to Talk

Lawrence F. Karr

Sound was not really sudden in its arrival on the screen. There was experimentation with the talking picture for years prior to Al Jolson's few songs and sparse dialogue in the Warner Brothers Vitaphone smash, THE JAZZ SINGER. Vitaphone itself would be replaced by a more sophisticated system; it was a stage in an evolution that began long before that nonetheless magical 1927 night at Warners Theatre in New York—and continued for some time after it.

The introduction of Edison's peep-show Kinetoscope in 1894 prompted him to attempt the wedding of movies to his phonograph, which had been invented in 1877. Such a combination of moving pictures and "synchronized" sound, the Kinetophone, was actually introduced a year later, but fewer than fifty of the machines were sold, and it met with commercial failure.

Nonetheless, considerable experimentation was to follow, with various processes appearing in the next thirty years, both in this country and abroad. A 1913 Edison film called JACK'S JOKE in the Library of Congress collection utilizes a crude synchronization of a projector with a phonograph record. A copy of experimental tests by J. T. Tykociner of the University of Illinois made in 1921, also in the collection, provides an example of early attempts to have sound placed directly on film.

The development of talking pictures which would be commercially practical for a mass audience was an undertaking which was perhaps even more complicated than the original development of moving pictures. The basic task of providing music, singing, and dialogue, loud and clear enough so as to be understandable to a theatre audience, required concurrent advancements in knowledge of sound itself, of theatre and recording acoustics (an unknown art), of sound optical systems and stabilized projection speeds, of adequate loudspeakers, and most important of all, of an amplifier capable of producing undistorted sound.

All of these developments were taking place slowly, until World War I inspired advances in electrical communications, leaving a vast confusion of claims and patents in the hands of giant companies such as

Franklin D. Roosevelt nominates Al Smith at the 1924 Democratic Convention.

Weber and Fields in a pool hall routine (De Forest, 1922).

 shows on the filmstrip margin the text "EASTM"

Westinghouse, General Electric, AT&T and its subsidiaries Bell Telephone and Western Electric, as well as in the hands of a number of independent inventors. Chief among these was Lee De Forest, whose invention of the audion amplifier tube in 1906 was to be the keystone of practical talking pictures. De Forest, who had made leading contributions to wireless telegraphy and radio, has been aptly called "the father of radio," and had himself envisioned talking pictures as early as 1900.

De Forest had begun work on sound-on-film talking pictures in 1913, but was forced to defer this experimentation for five years due to the pressure of his work with radio. Returning to this research in 1918, he gradually perfected a system of recording sound directly onto film, a process which is basically the same as that used today. In 1922, De Forest Phonofilms was incorporated and went into the business of producing synchronized sound-on-film talking pictures.

These films did not meet with great success, and might have been lost were it not for the efforts of Maurice H. Zouary, an independent film and television producer who carefully assembled through the years a collection of over a hundred reels of Phonofilm negatives and prints, including De Forest patent reels, papers, and other documents, and presented them to The American Film Institute Collection. These provide a fascinating record of the 1922-1927 period, and include such items as the first sound drama—a two-reel subject with Una Merkel called LOVE'S OLD SWEET SONG—and short films of stage musicals, minstrel shows, and vaudeville and early radio performers like Eddie Cantor, George Jessel, Molly Picon, Chic Sale, DeWolfe Hopper (reciting "Casey at the Bat"), Fannie Ward, and comedy teams like Weber & Fields and Bard & Pearl. Sound newsreels were introduced in 1924 with a campaign speech by Senator Robert La Follette and a talk by President Coolidge on the White House lawn.

De Forest did some of his work in a loose collaboration with Theodore Case and Earl Sponable, who eventually left and began working on improvements to De Forest's system by themselves. While De Forest was concentrating on producing and marketing his Phonofilms, Case and Sponable were improving his system until they were able to sell it to William Fox in 1926. It was christened Movietone, and became the backbone of Fox Movietone News and the Fox talking picture system. De Forest eventually sued Fox for infringement of his patents and after years of litigation received a relatively small sum for his work.

In the meantime, scientists at the Bell Telephone Laboratories had been working on a sophisticated version of the Edison Kinetophone, and synchronized a movie projector with a phonograph record, utilizing De Forest's amplifier, which he had licensed to AT&T for use with telephone and telegraph. Bell Telephone tried, without success, to sell its system to the major film companies, who rejected it as being a too complicated, expensive, and untried undertaking which wasn't needed by the industry since good money was still being made on silent pictures. It was Warner Brothers who, facing financial ruin in their competition with the major studios which controlled exhibition in first-run houses, bought the exclusive rights to the system and renamed it the Vitaphone process.

Thus, in August of 1926, more than three years after De Forest had first publicly demonstrated his Phono-film system, Warners opened DON JUAN in New York City, immediately before the Fox Movietone system was introduced. The all-synchronous sound program consisted of a prologue with Will Hays introducing the Vitaphone system, followed by musical numbers and operatic arias. DON JUAN itself was accompanied with a synchronized musical score by the New York Philharmonic Orchestra. But it was to be more than a year before limited dialogue and singing would be heard in a feature film (THE JAZZ SINGER, October, 1927) and over twenty months before the first all-talkie (LIGHTS OF NEW YORK).

THE JAZZ SINGER had less than 300 spoken words, but it caught the audiences' imagination as none of the earlier sound efforts had been able to do. Within two years a pell-mell race to re-equip theatres and rewire the Hollywood studios for sound was started.

Warner Brothers concentrated on using its Vitaphone system to make about 1,000 one and two-reel shorts between 1926 and 1931 (when the sound-on-disc system was finally scrapped in favor of industrywide standardization to sound-on-film). These shorts com-

The Yorke and Adams vaudeville team (De Forest, 1923).

Una Merkel in LOVE'S OLD SWEET SONG, *a 1924 De Forest featurette.*

77

Eva Puck and Sammy White (De Forest, 1922).

prised musical numbers by violinist Albert Spalding, Metropolitan Opera stars Giovanni Martinelli, Marion Talley, Jeanne Gordon, and Giuseppe De Luca, as well as playlets and dramatic monologues featuring silent stars William Boyd and H. B. Walthall; or Rin-Tin-Tin with his trainer, plus boxing celebrities Primo Carnera, James J. Corbett, Georges Carpentier, and Max Schmeling. Vitaphone filmed Fred Allen in 1929, Jack Benny the year before, and also offered comics Joe E. Brown, Bert Lahr, and Jack Haley. Radio and ballroom bands captured on film included Xavier Cugat's "Gigolos," Fred Waring's "Pennsylvanians," and Rudy Vallee's "Connecticut Yankees." Among the early radio personalities filmed were singers Kate Smith, Frank Crumit, and Julia Sanderson, and songwriter Harry Von Tilzer.

Historically speaking, the rush to make talking pictures created an invaluable record of celebrated cabaret, radio, Broadway, concert and opera personalities of the late twenties which otherwise would have survived only in memory. Unfortunately, while there are over 500 Vitaphone shorts in the AFI Collection, only the picture negatives have as yet been located. The fragile Vitaphone discs, physically separated from the film, were lost over the years. Thus, the search for films has been broadened to include these sound tracks, which hopefully survive in private hands on sixteen-inch phonograph discs bearing the Vitaphone label.

Dr. Lee De Forest exhibiting a strip of his sound film (1922).

Abbie Mitchell, performing for De Forest Phonofilms in 1923.

Part of a theatre trailer for an early sound film.

Tom Shales

Warners Musicals— Busby and Beyond

Busby Berkeley directing a musical number in DAMES, 1934. Ruby Keeler is in the center foreground.

The probable and mercifully uncomplicated reason for the survival of the movie musical is that it makes people feel good. Its longevity testifies to the cinema's capacity for escapist fantasy, for no matter how "realistic" musicals got to be in recent years, the moment anybody on-screen started singing, they became reassuringly surreal once again. For musicals, there has been more than one golden era—the MGM classics of the fifties, the Astaire-Rogers RKO alliance of the thirties—but musicals were never more ecstatic and shamelessly opulent than during the thirties at Warners—the Busby Berkeley era. In addition to the Berkeley films preserved in the AFI Collection, however, there are also musicals from the earliest days of sound and from the Warners forties, all of them attesting to the durability of the old song and dance.

There was music at Warner Brothers long before there was Busby Berkeley. In fact, a whole era of movie musicals came and went while Berkeley was still working in New York, along the Old Broadway he would later romanticize in his elaborate production numbers. United Artists, which owns the television rights to Warner Brothers sound films made prior to the fifties, has donated the original negative material for all these films, a number of which are musicals, to The American Film Institute Collection. The musicals in this United Artists—Warner Brothers Collection prove that movies, after all, did not so much learn to talk as they learned to sing.

The first "talkie," Warners' THE JAZZ SINGER (1927, Alan Crosland), had more singing than talking. Technical limitations of the Vitaphone sound-on-disc process made it easier to record music than spoken dialogue. Musicals seemed to make the most use of the new toy anyway, and the bandwagon which Warners started rolling soon had every studio in town as followers.

Berkeley's decision to migrate from Broadway to Hollywood was actually a belated response to an already rampant trend. Broadway stars and almost-stars had been flocking to the coast to perform in sound films and to quench the corporate thirst for musical movies. Many of the musicals that resulted from this

80

Dick Powell and Ruby Keeler in "Flirtation Walk."

Johnny Arthur and Louise Fazenda in THE DESERT SONG, 1929.

gold rush—often completed in only a few weeks—were by various standards dreadful; yet some are marked with flashes of invention, many contain imperishable performances by celebrated entertainers, most are tellingly evocative of the period in which they were made, and all of them together comprise a significant moment in film history.

These first musicals were often just stage shows, lifted out of a New York theatre and plopped down in front of a California camera, which sat there motionless as the parade pranced by. Big Broadway stars like Marilyn Miller came to movieland to recreate starring roles in films like SALLY (1929), for salaries like $1,000 an hour (for a total of 100 hours). Miss Miller's film was a great success, and she stayed on at Warners to make two more—SUNNY (1930), in which she sang, "Look for the Silver Lining" (later the title of her musical biography, filmed by Warners in 1949 with June Haver, and also in the Collection), and HER MAJESTY, LOVE (1931), which co-starred W. C. Fields.

SALLY benefitted from a more mobile camera than its predecessors. "Shooting to playback," then an innovation, meant that a song could be pre-recorded, freeing the singer from the repressions dealt by early and unwieldy recording equipment and microphones. That helped SALLY shed the shackles of the stage. Like many films—especially musicals—of the time, SALLY had sequences in the two-color Technicolor process. Musicals were advertised not only as "All Talking," "All Singing," and "All Dancing," but also on occasion as "All Color"—or at least part color, like Warners' THE DESERT SONG (1929) and THE GOLD DIGGERS OF BROADWAY (1929), a film that grossed more than three million dollars and of course launched a subgenre that Berkeley would noisily revive.

More than sixty films contained color sequences in 1929, and Warners released the first all-color talkie, a musical, the same year—ON WITH THE SHOW (which also marked the screen debut of Ethel Waters). Like innumerable musicals of the time, it was a backstage tears-and-smiles saga. Miss Waters enriches it with two memorable songs: "Birmingham Bertha" and "Am I Blue?" Meanwhile, Warners and other studios were calling on their big stars to sing—whether they were singers or not. Marion Davies, Ramon Novarro, Mary Pickford, and Clara Bow were all drafted. If you absolutely positively could not carry a tune, you could still be in a production number: Richard Barthelmess had his singing voice dubbed by somebody else, a tradition that movie musicals would uphold for many years to come.

Some of the early musicals were like television variety shows. Warners' SHOW OF SHOWS (1929)—the title would later be used, in fact, for a television variety show—was a collection of acts by big stars: John Barrymore read Shakespeare, Beatrice Lillie cut up. Other studios did their own versions—Paramount had PARAMOUNT ON PARADE (1930), and Universal released one of the most popular of all the revue films, KING OF JAZZ (1930), with Paul Whiteman, his band, and the Rhythm Boys, a vocal trio dominated by Harry Lillis "Bing" Crosby. The revue format did not completely die with the twenties. Warners revived it during the forties with its HOLLYWOOD CANTEEN (1944), featuring Joan Leslie, Bette Davis, and Roy Rogers, who sang Cole Porter's "Don't Fence Me In," while the late Trigger did some fancy hoofing; and THANK YOUR LUCKY STARS (1943), with Miss Davis singing "They're Either Too Young or Too Old," a cameo by Humphrey Bogart, a song by Dinah Shore, a tap dance by Ida Lupino, and other Warners stars, who did their things while Eddie Cantor and S. Z. "Cuddles" Sakall stumbled through a minimal plot, with Cantor playing himself. Both these films are in the Collection.

The early musicals also took the form of filmed operetta, represented at Warners by such titles as GOLDEN DAWN (1930), SONG OF THE FLAME (1930), KISS ME AGAIN (1931), and VIENNESE NIGHTS (1930), which Sigmund Romberg wrote directly for the screen, not the stage. Typical of this genre was THE DESERT SONG (1929), directed by Roy Del Ruth and starring the porcelain-voiced John Boles as Red Shadow, a sheik-like Robin Hood of Araby. The film is rather hesitantly sound—even its songs are occasionally interrupted for old-fashioned printed titles to advance the plot or set a location or describe a character. The cast also included Myrna Loy, delightfully incongruous as a seductive Azuri,

A tableau from ROMAN SCANDALS, 1933.

Una Merkel, Ruby Keeler, Warner Baxter and Ginger Rogers in 42ND STREET, 1933.

the hot-blooded half-caste, and Johnny Arthur, who made something of a career out of playing the stereotyped homosexual (or, at least sissy) in much the same way Willie Best made a career out of playing the stereotyped black. Arthur's role in this film is Benny Kidd, society reporter for the *Paris Herald*, who, when captured by the Riffs and threatened with bodily harm, snaps, "Don't be so effeminate! Where do you think you are—in Chicago?" Arthur was comic relief inserted at regular intervals. The hilarity included such exchanges as this one (with Louise Fazenda):

He: Why do secretaries always fall in love with the men they work for?

She: Well, if you're going to let a man dictate to you, you might as well marry him.

Mordaunt Hall, reviewing THE DESERT SONG for *The New York Times*, was impressed by the film's color "flashes" and John Boles' singing, but complained that "the characters . . . seem to seize upon song at inopportune moments." It was this fatal proclivity which probably sealed the doom of the early movie musical. Audiences wearied of that eternal effervescence and probably sensed the fact that most of these movies were decidedly uncinematic. At any rate, a public that once responded eagerly to the old song-and-dance now snubbed the musical, and theatre managers coaxed them indoors with promises that the current attraction did not have a song in its heart or anywhere else.

The work of Busby Berkeley has been described as everything from purest cinema to fascist fantasy. Whatever Berkeley's excesses—and they could be excessive—he was an original, and proud of it. He created a vocabulary for the musical film that did not depend on the logistics of the stage, although ironically most of his thirties musicals pretended that the outlandish concoctions he invented were in fact taking place on a stage in front of a live audience. The audience was seen only at the beginning and end of these sequences, however, so they could be forgotten. One's imagination could soar along with Busby into the Berkeley void, where girls might pop up, or down, or out of virtually anywhere, doing virtually anything, but always in rhythm and usually in a symmetrical pattern.

Ruby Keeler (center) in "The Shadow Waltz" production number from GOLD DIGGERS OF 1933.

May McAvoy and Al Jolson in THE JAZZ SINGER, 1927.

James Cagney (on table) in the "Shanghai Lil" production number from FOOTLIGHT PARADE, *1933.*

Berkeley did not direct all or most of the Warners films that he's famous for. He was usually billed as choreographer, though he likes to brag now that he never took a dance lesson in his life. What he did was, of course, to choreograph the camera itself—to shake it loose from its moorings, take it up into the rafters for the by-now famous "top shot" or take it down under the sound stage, drilling holes and using mirrors for startling new perspectives. Berkeley once told *Cahiers du Cinéma*, "A great part of my work has not been the work of a choreographer strictly speaking, because, for me, if I dare to say it, it is the camera that must dance." In the same interview, Berkeley put his finger on the simple secret of his success: "The most surprising occurrences followed one another in my ballets in a way that was my own, and that was what the public liked. People have often asked me how I went about creating these effects, how the idea for them came to me, and I have never known how to answer. Not that I don't want to, but I just can't. I'm completely at a loss to explain my 'method.'" Once, at a screening of musical sequences from his films at the Gallery of Modern Art in New York, a student asked Berkeley if maybe he had been influenced by German Expressionism. "No," he said, smiling, "I never heard of it. Everything I did was my own."

We may tend to think of Berkeley numbers only in terms of mob scenes—a herd of white pianos, a squadron of scantily-clad cuties, a fleet of neon violins. But Berkeley always took note of the fact that those fly-specks down there, those things bobbing about in the water, were people. He says he was the first director to use close-ups of chorus girls in production numbers (in WHOOPEE, 1930, for Samuel Goldwyn), and Berkeley took great pains to cut to those faces in most of his future numbers. His art of cutting from the great to the small has been cited as one of the best reasons for calling him a genius. "I worked with human beings," he told a British interviewer. "It's from that you get the exhilaration. I'd always splash in a close-up to show that those lines of girls, those designs, were really human beings."

All of Berkeley's Warner Brothers films are in the AFI Collection, including the first musical he com-

Pert Kelton, Marilyn Miller and Joe E. Brown in SALLY, 1929.

Gordon MacRae and Doris Day in TEA FOR TWO, 1950.

pletely directed, GOLD DIGGERS OF 1935, which features two of his greatest numbers: "The Words Are in My Heart" and the super-surrealist "Lullaby of Broadway," Berkeley's oft-cited personal favorite and in every way a striking composition, from the distantly lit face of Wini Shaw that opens and closes it, to the nightclub that has 100 dancers and two customers, to the sudden plunge from a balcony that Berkeley used, say some, to announce the death of the "gold digger" Broadway baby (though he himself would work on two more "Gold Diggers" films). Among the other classic sequences Berkeley created are "The Shadow Waltz" (neon violins) from GOLD DIGGERS OF 1933; "Spin a Little Web of Dreams" (gondolas and ostrich feathers) from FASHIONS OF 1934; "The Lady in Red" from IN CALIENTE (1935); "Those Beautiful Dames" and "I Only Have Eyes for You" from DAMES (1934); and two gems from FOOTLIGHT PARADE (1933): "By a Waterfall," with its rising-fountain aqua-ballet, and "Shanghai Lil," with James Cagney doing a pre-YANKEE DOODLE DANDY tap dance with Ruby Keeler after smoky shots of Oriental prostitutes lounging in satin. The number ends with marching men, shot from overhead, forming pictures of Franklin D. Roosevelt and the National Relief Act, We-Do-Our-Part Eagle.

But in addition to the well-known Berkeleys—42ND STREET (1933) and the others—the Collection includes less-remembered titles like GO INTO YOUR DANCE (1935), the only movie Ruby Keeler made with then-husband Al Jolson; BRIGHT LIGHTS (1935, Berkeley) with Joe E. Brown; I LIVE FOR LOVE (1935, Berkeley) with Dolores Del Rio; STARS OVER BROADWAY (1935, William Keighley) with James Melton and Jane Froman; STAGE STRUCK (1936, Berkeley) with Dick Powell and Joan Blondell; COMET OVER BROADWAY (1938, Berkeley) with Kay Francis; and Berkeley's non-musical directorial assignment, THEY MADE ME A CRIMINAL (1939), with John Garfield, Claude Rains, Ann Sheridan, Leo Gorcey, and Huntz Hall, no less.

Just as the Warners musical did not begin with Berkeley, so it doesn't end with his passage to Fox and MGM in the forties. The Warners dominance of the genre may have been over, but the company continued to produce musicals, some of them exceptional. In the forties they included Irving Rapper's superior biography RHAPSODY IN BLUE (1945), the story, approximately, of George Gershwin, and two films by Michael Curtiz: NIGHT AND DAY (1946), an inadequate Cole Porter biography saved by fine musical numbers; and ROMANCE ON THE HIGH SEAS (1948), arguably the best of the usually limpid Doris Day vehicles, with Jack Carson and, as a former Doris Day flame, Oscar Levant. Doris was twenty-four, it was her first starring role, and she sang, "It's Magic." One of the musical numbers, at least, had the consultant's touch of none other than Busby Berkeley. Other Warners musicals of the period had a kind of warmed-over, second-hand ennui like TEA FOR TWO (1950), a Doris Day remake of "No No, Nanette," and THE TIME, THE PLACE, AND THE GIRL (1946), with Dennis Morgan as a latter-day Dick Powell—only not latter enough.

There are many other Warners musicals in the AFI Collection. They range from the significant to the curious—from Al Jolson singing "Sonny Boy" in THE SINGING FOOL (1928, Lloyd Bacon) to a guest appearance by Bugs Bunny in MY DREAM IS YOURS (1949). In their finest moments, these musicals were sublime, providing a vicarious liberation unique to the genre and conveying an innocence that may never be duplicated.

PATHS TO PARADISE

Pamela C. Wintle

Famous Players-Lasky. 1925.
Director: Clarence Badger.
Screenplay: Keene Thompson.
Cast: Raymond Griffith, Betty Compson, Tom Santschi,
Bert Woodruff, Fred Kelsey.

*In film history, there have been many victims of
progress and many worthy artists lost in shuffles.
Raymond Griffith had the dubious distinction of being
both of these—his acting career ended when sound
arrived, because he had no voice, and his silent pan-
tomimes have been unjustly overlooked in the zeal
with which we view the work of Chaplin, Keaton, and
their illustrious contemporaries. In a sense, Raymond
Griffith is alive and well—on film—and awaiting his
rescue from oblivion.*

Overshadowed by the great comedians of the twenties
—Chaplin, Keaton, Lloyd, and Langdon—Raymond
Griffith is remembered by only a handful of film buffs
and historians. He was born into a theatrical family
in Boston, and as a youth is said to have lost his
voice shrieking nightly in the melodrama "The Witch-
ing Hour," though it is more likely that bronchial
pneumonia was the cause. Since Griffith's speech was
barely above a hoarse whisper, he was forced to seek
other employment; and with a dance background and
a natural inclination for pantomime, he found a job
touring the vaudeville circuits with a French mime
company.

In time he found another natural outlet for his
talents—silent films. He began with Vitagraph in 1914,
and, switching to Keystone, he worked up through
the ranks to become Sennett's assistant. With FORTY
WINKS in 1925, he achieved his right to star status
and his own comedy series for Paramount. (Griffith's
acting career was another victim of the coming of
sound. His last part was that of a dying French sol-
dier in ALL QUIET ON THE WESTERN FRONT.
He then continued in Hollywood as a writer and
producer.)

The film that followed FORTY WINKS, PATHS
TO PARADISE, confirmed not only his stardom but
clearly demonstrated that Griffith could attain the
heights of the comedy masters.

As an actor, Griffith adopted as his trademark (like
Max Linder) the appearance of a suave gentleman
who, from morning till night, is dressed in formal
attire. Thus he became known as the "silk hat comedian." This well-bred character, the essence of charm

Betty Compson and Raymond Griffith in PATHS TO PARADISE.

and self-confidence, never becomes unruffled even in the most desperate situations. Griffith's early training is evident from his graceful movements, the inclusion of pantomime, and a theatrical flair for the smallest detail. And—most disarming—a smile that could sweeten the sourest disposition.

PATHS TO PARADISE, by the fine comedy director Clarence Badger, is a totally implausible film but, as noted in *Moving Picture World* (July 11, 1925), "... nothing short of paralysis of the facial muscles will prevent your laughter."

The film opens in a San Francisco dive where Molly (Betty Compson) and her pals cater to the curious tourists seeking a glimpse of the underworld. The dive converts to an opium den for a sharply dressed Griffith, who appears to be an easy mark. The incidents happen quickly, and he is led to believe he has shot a man. Horrified, he is relieved to learn one of the men is willing to accept the blame for $500. He pays the money but as he leaves, a twist occurs. Griffith taps on the door, a friend enters, and Griffith turns and flashes a sly smile—and also a badge. The gang offers Griffith a bribe, and with a magnificent display of reluctance, communicated only by his back shoulder movements, Griffith agrees to accept the return of his $500—plus a bonus. With the departure of Griffith and friend, Molly finds Griffith's badge which is inscribed "Gas Meter Inspector."

Molly and Griffith meet again in a hotel lobby where he is answering to different names being paged by bellboys. Events lead both of them to a party at the home of a kind and wealthy man where a diamond described as somewhat smaller than the "rock of Gibraltar," a gift to his daughter, is being guarded. Griffith comes as a guest under an assumed name, of course, and Molly has found employment as a maid. They compete against each other for the diamond tucked away in a small safe, but admiration leads to an alliance. The sequence of attempts—and there are many—allows Griffith full play with his character. There are many close shaves in which he never loses his cool demeanor. With safe in hand, he even maintains calm when a detective wrestles with a dog gripping a flashlight in his teeth that spotlights Griffith wherever he moves in the room.

They do steal the diamond and find themselves racing toward the border with every motorcycle policeman en route chasing them. The chase is one of the best. Every maneuver elicits a gasp from the audience. Finally Molly and Griffith bounce across the border to safety yards ahead of the law. So ends reel 6; reel 7 had deteriorated when The American Film Institute obtained the nitrate print. But the script indicates that reel 7 is an equally thrilling chase *back* to San Francisco to return the diamond. Molly and Griffith are forgiven, and they drive off to be married and to seek a life of honesty.

The RKO Shorts

Leonard Maltin

How did people learn how to make movies when movies—and later talkies—were young? There weren't all that many veterans around to give lessons—basically, everybody was a novice. But there were such institutions as the RKO short subject unit, where young and aspiring actors, directors, cameramen, and writers could break into the business and learn the craft. And the shorts themselves, preserved today, not only reveal the birth pangs of young talent but also evoke an era when millions of Americans embraced "the movies" as their major source of entertainment.

The RKO short-subject unit had all the advantages and none of the disadvantages of being allied with a major Hollywood studio. It was an invaluable training ground for actors, directors, cameramen, and writers; if they showed promise, they were graduated to feature films. Studio sets, costumes, and facilities were available for use by the short-subject people, so their product always had an expensive look that many rival shorts lacked.

One director who made good in the department was Mark Sandrich. He worked with stage stars Clark and McCullough, imposing his flair for slapstick on Bobby Clark's masterful use of dialogue in such shorts as THE ICEMAN'S BALL (which featured a young Walter Brennan) and THE GAY NIGHTIES. Then Sandrich directed a bizarre three-reel musical with Phil Harris called SO THIS IS HARRIS. In addition to rhythmic dialogue, new songs, and a standard comedy plot featuring Walter Catlett, it had a dazzling display of camera gyrations—this at a time when the filming techniques of short subjects were rather prosaic.

The short won an Academy Award that year, 1933. RKO executives were so impressed, they let Sandrich direct a feature, MELODY CRUISE, duplicating the style of the short (and starring Phil Harris). He went on to direct the classic Fred Astaire-Ginger Rogers films (THE GAY DIVORCEE, TOP HAT), for which he is best remembered.

George Stevens came to RKO after spending many years with Hal Roach; with him came Grady Sutton, to star in Stevens' new series, "The Blondes and the Redheads," with Carol Tevis and June Brewster. The

Leon Errol and Dorothy Christy in DOUBLE UP, 1943.

Clark and McCullough in ALIBI BYE BYE, 1935.

Florence Lake, George Stevens, and Edgar Kennedy celebrate the third anniversary of Edgar Kennedy's comedy series at RKO.

real characters whom audiences came to regard as old friends. Of the 103 two-reelers in the series, several stand out: DUMMY ACHE (featuring Lucille Ball); WRONG DIRECTION, in which Edgar has a chance to become a movie director until his family visits the set; DUMB'S THE WORD, in which he has to dig a tunnel to reach a pot of gold buried in his neighbor's yard; and HOME CANNING, in which the family "borrows" a neighbor's kitchen to jar some preserves and makes a shambles of the place.

Leon Errol rose to fame on the Broadway stage with his rubber-legs routine; when he started making shorts, he fell into a pattern of farcical comedy involving a perennially jealous wife. This was the basis for most of his two-reelers; he made eighty-nine in all for RKO between 1934 and his death in 1951.

His initial comedies, however, were vaudeville-oriented, written and directed by famed gagman Al Boasberg. Such two-reelers as DOWN THE RIBBER are classic examples of vaudeville patter routines. Of his later marital farces, two stand out: DOUBLE UP, in which Leon hires a look-alike to stay home with his wife while he goes out with the boys, and BLONDES AWAY, the archetypical blonde-in-the-closet comedy. A 1938 entry, THE JITTERS, preserves his classic rubber-legs routine on film.

From the mid-forties on, veteran Hal Roach staffer Hal Yates wrote and directed nearly all the Kennedy and Errol comedies, adding a consistency and brisk pacing they had lacked before.

Throughout the years, RKO constantly came up with unusual shorts that really went off the beaten path. The musicals ranged from country-western outings with Ray Whitley to miniature musical comedies with Ruth Etting, as well as a quota of "big band" shorts and one or two films featuring Betty Grable. In the late forties, RKO tried a boy-and-his-dog series starring Ted Donaldson.

RKO always turned out a slick, professional product; many of the shorts were photographed by such notable cameramen as Nicholas Musuraca and Ted McCord. Even in the fifties, when RKO continued to make shorts with Gil Lamb and "The Newlyweds," the look of quality that had always characterized the studio's two-reelers remained intact.

first short in the series, FLIRTING IN THE PARK, showed the Hal Roach influence in its style and in its build-up to a hilarious debacle by a lake in the park. Stevens' handling of these comedies and several with Edgar Kennedy won him a chance to direct feature-length comedies with Wheeler and Woolsey for the studio, such as KENTUCKY KERNELS and THE NITWITS (also in the AFI Collection).

RKO's longest-running series starred Edgar Kennedy and Leon Errol. Kennedy was already well-established when he inaugurated his series in 1931, but these domestic two-reelers boosted his popularity and made his slow-burn routine (rubbing his face in frustration) famous. Featuring Florence Lake as his scatterbrained wife with a mile-a-minute mouth, the Kennedy comedies flourished for seventeen years until Kennedy's death in 1948.

They set a pattern for situation comedy that was taken up by television in the early fifties: an audience will accept comic exaggeration if the basis for the comedy is real. Kennedy and Florence Lake created

William Beaudine

Kevin Brownlow

Excavation for lost or forgotten films can turn up lost or forgotten filmmakers, too. William Beaudine was not precisely lost nor exactly forgotten, but he was severely underestimated until AFI unearthed such silent Beaudines as PENROD AND SAM and THE CANADIAN. Not even Beaudine himself had seen much of his silents since the days of their release. On viewing THE CANADIAN decades later, he said, "I'm very surprised. Why, I was quite a good director in spots." That was understatement, but the director's pleasure in rediscovering himself was shared by the audience that watched the movie with him. A record was in the process of being set straight.

William Beaudine is remembered today chiefly for his extended directorial work on the television series "Lassie." However, Beaudine began his career as a property boy at Biograph, and by the twenties he was directing such silent classics as LITTLE ANNIE ROONEY (1925), SPARROWS (1926), PENROD AND SAM (1923), and, newly rediscovered, THE CANADIAN (1926).

THE CANADIAN was an uncharacteristic film for Beaudine—an adaptation of Somerset Maugham's play "The Land of Promise."

*   *   *

To the Canadian wheat fields comes Nora Marsh (Mona Palma, previously known as a child star under the name of Mimi Palmeri). The death of an aunt she lived with in London had robbed her of her security, and she intends to stay with her brother Edward (Wyndham Standing). Her previous traveling being confined to Paris and the Riviera, she has no conception of frontier life. Frank Taylor (Thomas Meighan, one of the most intelligent and reliable of silent actors), a homesteader working for Marsh, picks her up from the station. She is cool and elegant, frosty toward Taylor, and quite hopelessly out of place in this rough farming country. Reaching her brother's farm, she shows her horror of the rawness of the place and the people, making an instant enemy of her brother's wife, Gertie (Dale Fuller). The arrival

Mona Palma alienates her hosts by cleaning her fork in THE CANADIAN, 1926.

THE CANADIAN

Famous Players-Lasky. 1926.
Director: William Beaudine.
Adaptation: Arthur Stringer, based on the play, "The Land of Promise" by William Somerset Maugham.
Cast: Thomas Meighan, Mona Palma, Wyndham Standing, Dale Fuller, Charles Winninger, Billy Butts.

Mona Palma and Thomas Meighan in THE CANADIAN.

scene is treated with a rare sense of observation; as the beautiful Nora takes her place at the meal table, awkwardness overcomes the men. Frank Taylor fails to stand up, and Nora glares at him. She wipes her knife and fork on her napkin and succeeds in alienating Gertie and Frank with that one movement. The situation is conveyed with surreptitious glances and brief gestures.

When threshing begins, Nora feels she might be useful in the kitchen, but she simply infuriates Gertie, who hands her a saucepan and tells her to put some rice in it. Nora drops the lid of the rice jar and pours it all in. Not knowing any better, she places the saucepan on the stove, and the rice is soon boiling over disastrously.

"Can't you do anything?" asks Gertie. "You've wasted enough for fifty men."

At the next meal, the men have returned more or less to their normal style of conversation. Taylor talks of getting a squaw for a wife to clean and sew. "I hope I have better luck than Penny Simpson. She broke a leg and he had to shoot her!"

Taylor and his pal roar with laughter. Cut to grim Nora. She gets up.

"I'm not accustomed to such talk about marriage," says Nora, icily.

"Fine wife you'd make," spits Gertie. "You can't even boil rice."

Taking a deep breath, Nora preserves her sang-froid: "You forget, I didn't have the advantage of an early training as a servant."

Gertie explodes with wrath at this sarcasm, and a full-scale row blows up. "I don't care if she *is* your sister," she tells her husband, who tries hard to keep everyone on an even keel. "She's going to apologize to me."

Edward Marsh has to persuade his sister to do so, and the clash of wills leads her to seek a desperate solution to get away. She approaches Frank Taylor: "You said you needed a wife to clean and sew. Will I do?"

The remainder of the film is an intimate study of the conflict between these two people, married against their will, managing hardly to be civil to each other.

It is one of the most difficult kinds of pictures to

make—basically two people in one room. Beaudine does not resort to imposed drama to help him, nor to a glossy style. He sets his camera on a close-shot, and lets the characters say everything through facial expression and gesture. Not for a moment are the performances exaggerated; Beaudine makes his actors behave like human beings.

Shortly after screening THE CANADIAN, I went to interview Beaudine and was surprised to learn that he had not seen any of his silent films since their release; in some cases, he failed to see them even then, due to the pressure of work. After I described my delight with THE CANADIAN, Beaudine replied casually, "Yes, I did that in '26 up in Canada. We had the damndest luck on that. We went up to Canada in September and our story was about this wheat farmer (Meighan) and he was struggling like the dickens to get along, and he had this great wheat field. And the bother of it was that an ungodly snowstorm came and put the wheat down flat. Well, we wondered how the hell we were going to get that. They had planned to bring a lot of wheat to the studio. And I'll be damned if in the middle of September, up in Calgary, Canada, if it didn't snow. And after we had photographed the wheat field as it was, we wake up next morning and there's about a foot of snow out there. So we dashed right out and photographed it. I don't know what's left in the picture, but that's the way it happened. And we didn't have to do a damned thing but photograph it.

"We had a great time on that trip. We went from here to New York, from New York to Calgary, went back to New York, saw all the World Series games—nobody worked those days!—and came back to California, all expenses paid. I was paid from the time I got in the train till I got off here, and I was getting $2,500 a week at the time, and $200 a week living expenses on top of that. So I was in good shape."

Beaudine confessed that he'd never seen THE CANADIAN. Why was he given such a serious dramatic subject in the first place? "I'll tell you why I got THE CANADIAN to do. I was a comedy director essentially. I was getting to the end of my contract with Warners—a contract from '22 to '26—and they had been making money. My top salary was $1,750,

and they were renting me out at $2,500 a week, and with nothing for me to do. And they said, 'Well, how'd you like to go to New York and do a picture for Paramount?' I said, 'Fine. What the hell? I'd sooner work than sit around here.' So they'd rent me to Paramount at $2,500 a week. I had a nice clause in my contract that I got half the profit—I shared on the $750 that they made profit. So I didn't care. I got my expenses and my living expenses, and first class transportation for me and my wife. It just happened that it was getting to the end of my contract, and they sent me back to do a comedy with Richard Dix. On the way back there, Paramount changed their minds, and since they were stuck with the contract, they put me on THE CANADIAN which was an entirely different kind of thing from what I'd been doing. But Bill LeBaron was running it back in New York, and he was quite a nice guy. We got along fine, and I did a fairly good picture with it, and they were satisfied."

"Did you ever work on a farm in your life?" I asked.

"No."

*　　　*　　　*

The season of early films which had opened The American Film Institute Theatre in Washington came to the Los Angeles County Museum of Art. As soon as the print of THE CANADIAN arrived, we tried to persuade Beaudine to come to a private screening.

"I'd like to see it very much," he said, "but I've had the flu and it just won't go away. It affects my legs. Give me a call in a day or two. I'll see how I feel."

In a day or two, he was no better. The night of the performance came round, and there was no chance of his arriving to introduce the film. The house was packed. No one had heard of THE CANADIAN, and no one particularly wanted to see it. The crowds had come for the main feature, the legendary musical, BROADWAY (Paul Fejos). Shortly before his film was due to start, Beaudine arrived—in a wheelchair. His son had arranged for him to be present. The Head of Special Programs at the museum, Philip Chamberlin, was delighted; would he say a few words before

Mona Palma, Wyndham Standing, and Thomas Meighan in THE CANADIAN.

the film?

"Not on your life," said Beaudine. "I'll wait till I've seen it."

THE CANADIAN was the hit of the evening. The audience applauded during the picture, and they applauded at the end. And then—and only then—did Beaudine agree to talk. He was wheeled to the front of the theatre.

"I'm very surprised," he said. "Why—I was quite a good director in spots."

The audience gave him a standing ovation.

Convinced that Beaudine would not attend the show, I managed to miss this whole dramatic incident. But he described it for me afterwards on the telephone. "Jesus," he said, "that did my ego a hell of a lot of good. I feel like a prima donna. Now see what you can do about finding PENROD AND SAM."

         *   *   *

I had given up PENROD AND SAM as one of those tantalizing pictures that had crumbled to dust in the vaults, when it came to light in one of the AFI's searches. The tinted 35mm print was in good shape. Ben Alexander, featured by Griffith in HEARTS OF THE WORLD as an infant and the portly detective of "Dragnet" in the 1950s, plays Penrod; Joe Butterworth, his friend Sam; Rockliffe Fellowes, his father; and Gladys Brockwell, his mother.

The picture was perfectly described in *Photoplay* Magazine's enthusiastic review (August, 1923): "It is delightful in its un-screen qualities, a fresh and diverting study of the small boy rampant. It wasn't easy to develop a series of episodic adventures into a well-knit scenario, but the present adapters seem to have overcome most of the difficulties. . . . (The scenario was by Hope Loring and Louis Lighton from Booth Tarkington's stories.) No attempt is made towards punches—and yet PENROD AND SAM achieves a highly moving moment in the death of the boy's pet dog. Here is tragedy unadulterated. Director William Baudine (*sic*) has told all these boyish episodes with a gentle and understanding adroitness, and he has been aided by a very satisfying cast. . . . It is interesting to note that along with other moves towards naturalism, all makeup was discarded. There are no beaded eyelashes and cupid-bow lips."

I remembered Beaudine's explanation of his facility with children—"Well, I had kids of my own; I understood kids"—and decided I'd try for a more convincing explanation. I telephoned his home, but there was no reply. Before arranging a screening, I tried his number again. No reply. Two days later, *Variety* ran this item on their front page: "Bill Beaudine, Sr., dies at 78, Eldest Active Director . . . among his earlier credits were LITTLE ANNIE ROONEY with Mary Pickford and Paramount's THE CANADIANS (*sic*) made in 1926, but only recently artistically credited as being one of the top films of that pre-sound period. At a recent showing of it in L.A. County Museum he got up after it was screened and said, 'Well, this is the first time in 44 years I ever had a chance to see it.'"

"They've gone and killed my Duke."

Tom Shales

ONLY ANGELS HAVE WINGS

Columbia Pictures. 1939.
Director and Producer: Howard Hawks.
Screenplay: Jules Furthman, based on a story by Howard Hawks.
Cast: Cary Grant, Jean Arthur, Richard Barthelmess,
Rita Hayworth, Thomas Mitchell, Noah Beery, Jr.

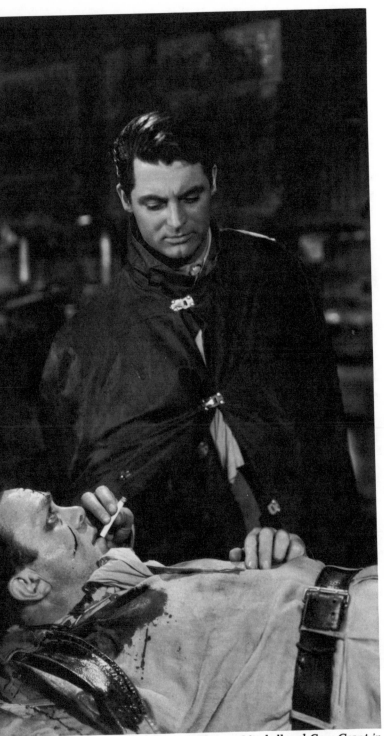

Thomas Mitchell and Cary Grant in
ONLY ANGELS HAVE WINGS.

Action is as American as—as American as anything. To the cry of "lights, camera, action," directors like Howard Hawks responded with an emphasis on the latter—not only physical action, but verbal action as well. His films aim at a target and hit it right on. Hawks, who would probably say he made movies, not films, contributed enormously to the development of the American film as an electric, kinetic, crowd-pleasing spectacle—a mirror image—revved up and roaring— of America itself.

Howard Hawks, wrote critic Pauline Kael, "represents the American commercial film at its best—fast, unpretentious, entertaining, with a sophisticated and 'hardboiled' attitude toward sex and money."

ONLY ANGELS HAVE WINGS, released by Columbia in 1939, lives up to that standard. Like many Hawks films, it is a story of men being manly and women standing by them. The men are matter-of-fact heroes; as pilots for a small mail carrying airline in tropical "Barranca," they risk their lives hourly without making much of a fuss. They scoff at danger and spit at death, and their attitude reflects that American reckless daring that survived the Depression, won the War, and still persists, if nowhere else, in the films of Howard Hawks.

It is testimony to Hawks' way with actors that the two leads in this film seem patently miscast yet are almost instantly acceptable—Cary Grant as the never-daunted airline boss and Jean Arthur as a visiting chorus girl, both of them far more Central Park South than swampy jungle; yet it scarcely matters.

Jules Furthman's screenplay, from a Hawks story, is a model of efficiency, not only in catching the story in motion and keeping it there, but in its effortless agility at establishing believable characters with minimal information and sparse, brittle dialogue. Furthman and Hawks were frequent, and perhaps ideal, collaborators; their styles were perfectly matched—straightforward, wisecracking, abruptly irreverent. When good old Joe dies in a plane crash, Grant and the other pilots refuse to mourn. "He just wasn't good enough," says Grant. "He was bound to get it sooner or later." When Grant and Miss Arthur are well into the sexual cat-and-mouse ritual almost obligatory to such adventure stories, the rites are cool and curt: He: "You're a queer duck." She: "So are you." He: "I can't figure you out." She: "Same here." End of love scene.

Like the best Hawks heroes, the men in this film prove their bravery without fanfare. The script erects almost every possible obstacle in the paths of the little airplanes: fog, storms, motors on fire, mountains, trees, a torn tail, and even a condor crashing through the windshield. When it is time to die, The Kid (Thomas Mitchell) notes casually, "I guess this is it, huh?" Yet beneath the flippancy of the characters, as beneath the "hardboiled" shell of the film itself, there lurks a strain of sentiment. According to the Hawks ethic, that sentiment derives mostly from the fellowship of men in danger together; women are, by and large, ineffectual bystanders or necessary nuisances.

Hawks has often been compared to John Ford. Their styles are similar. However, Hawks does not share Ford's more expansive historical vision, while Ford lacks the Hawks flare for dynamic, sophisticated comedy (HIS GIRL FRIDAY, TWENTIETH CENTURY). Like Ford, though, Hawks is most successful when remaining within the American experience (SCARFACE, RED RIVER) rather than venturing outside it (LAND OF THE PHARAOHS). At the 1970 Chicago International Film Festival, Hawks said that Ford "was a good director when I started, and I copied him every time I could." In fact, the Ford influence in ONLY ANGELS HAVE WINGS can be traced to Ford's AIR MAIL (1932), in which the plot and characterizations are too close to be coincidental.

To the same audience Hawks revealed the philosophy intrinsic to all his films but one. On the advice of a friend who saw his first film (THE ROAD TO GLORY, 1926) as catering to critics and not the public, his goal with every film since has been "to make entertainment," pure and, primarily, simple.

ONLY ANGELS HAVE WINGS—also notable as the first major screen appearance of Rita Hayworth—is not, thanks to television, a scarcely seen film. But because of Columbia Pictures' donation to The American Film Institute Collection at the Library of Congress, the availability of quality prints in the future and the permanence of one of Hawks' best works are insured.

Thomas Mitchell, Jean Arthur, and Cary Grant in
ONLY ANGELS HAVE WINGS.

Tom Shales

HIGH SIERRA

Warner Brothers. 1941.
Director: Raoul Walsh.
Screenplay: John Huston and W. R. Burnett, based on the novel
by W. R. Burnett.
Cast: Humphrey Bogart, Ida Lupino, Alan Curtis, Arthur Kennedy,
Joan Leslie, Henry Travers.

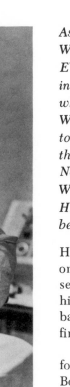

Henry Hull and Humphrey Bogart in HIGH SIERRA.

As a silent director, Raoul Walsh made the classic
WHAT PRICE GLORY? in 1926 and other features like
EVANGELINE (1919) and SADIE THOMPSON (1928),
in which he appeared with Gloria Swanson. But even
when he went on to sound films, his greatest successes,
Walsh remained a silent director to many. His rough-
tough, speeded-up, pragmatic artfulness was perhaps
thought too commercially proficient to qualify as art.
Now, through a reappraisal of Walsh works like
WHITE HEAT, THE ROARING TWENTIES, and
HIGH SIERRA, the vigor of his vivid cinema is
being recognized.

Humphrey Bogart gets the respectful star treatment
on his first appearance in HIGH SIERRA. First we
see his legs as he walks out of a prison gate, then
his arm as he gives a farewell handshake, then his
back as he looks at the prison he's leaving, and then,
finally, his face as he looks at the prison he's entering.

Director Raoul Walsh probably used the approach
for more than homage, because when we first see
Bogart we are slightly stunned; he looks old. His hair
has been tinted grey along the sides, and the prison
haircut, high above the ears, makes him look even
older. This is not to be, one could safely then assume,
quite the romantic odyssey other gangster pictures
were. For Roy Earle (Bogart), almost everything is
going to be downhill—even when he climbs to the top
of a mountain. It is there that he makes his final
stand, holding out for hopeless hours like the resisting
anachronism that he is. Walsh is mourning, to some
extent, the waning of a genre. Certainly gangsters did
not disappear from the screen. But they belonged to
the thirties, and the Walsh film, in 1941, seemed to
know it.

The gangster was in many ways the romantic hero
of his era, a kind of existential errant knight roaming
the empty plains of the Depression and managing to
survive through brute force and clear daring. As today
some airline hijackers and a few fabulous frauds grab
the public imagination, so in the twenties and thirties
the outlaw and his exploits became running serials in
the public press, with many people hoping, secretly
or otherwise, that the bandits would "get away."

Cornel Wilde, Arthur Kennedy, Humphrey Bogart, Alan Curtis, and Ida Lupino in HIGH SIERRA.

Arthur Kennedy, Ida Lupino, Alan Curtis, and Humphrey Bogart in HIGH SIERRA.

Theirs was a rootless, nomadic, exciting life, while the people reading the true-life gangster stories felt trapped, regimented, and bored.

John Huston and W. R. Burnett collaborated on the screenplay from a Burnett novel. As usual, the Walsh direction was smooth, efficient, and hypertense. There is little explicit violence, but there is violence in the air. The way Walsh people come at each other, verbally and emotionally, keeps things almost perpetually on edge. Walsh encourages the broad gesture and the italicized reaction in his characters; things run to extremes and hence become sometimes achingly vivid, yet never so stylized that credibility—on a certain special level—really suffers.

That technique is apparent, too, in another Walsh film in The American Film Institute Collection: ME AND MY GAL (1932, screenplay by Arthur Kober), with Spencer Tracy and Joan Bennett. Tracy is a gruff Irish cop on the waterfront, a kind of humanitarian tough guy whose way of settling a dispute between two little boys is to turn his back and urge them to slug it out. Walsh frequents low-life environments; here, there is spitting in faces, liberal drunkenness, and an old Irishman who looks right into the camera at the end of the film and says, "Well, it's all over. Come on, let's have another drink, huh?"

And there are the Walsh bits—a running-gag drunk (who becomes increasingly unfunny), a jabbering radio salesman, a turkey reduced to a skeleton by greedy wedding guests, and a Tracy crony who insists on acting as his echo. To punch up a love scene between Tracy and Bennett, Walsh has them first remark about love scenes in movies like STRANGE INTERLUDE where only the audience hears what the lovers are really thinking. Then, Walsh does the same bit—Bennett spurns a kiss but in voiceover we hear her thinking: "He kissed me, I'm so thrilled. But I'll pretend I'm mad." Tracy, after the kiss, thinks: "This dame didn't make much of a squawk about that kiss. Think I'll turn out the light and give her the works." She doesn't get the works, though. No matter how manly and rugged a Walsh hero, he expects his girl—his real girl—to be a virgin.

In HIGH SIERRA, Bogart develops an infatuation for a clubfooted girl who to him connotes purity and innocence. Ida Lupino, in a tough but sensitive portrayal, plays a former dime-a-dance tootsie named Marie Garson. She obviously really loves Roy Earle, but he tells her, "I'm givin' it to you straight. I got plans, see, and you don't fit into 'em. You could never mean nothin' to me. Nothin' special." Eventually, though, after Roy has paid to have the girl's clubfoot repaired, he finds out that she, too, is a tramp at heart, involved with a man back East who turns out to be an oily milquetoast. Roy will settle for Marie, another sign of his decline and fall as an American life style.

Just about everything conspires against Earle. He is given a dog that's a jinx (by comic reliefer—and racial stereotype—Willie Best). A wise gangster doctor (Henry Hull) tells him, "Remember what Johnny Dillinger said about guys like you—you're just rushin' toward death." The good old Dillinger heydays are over, and later, when Bogart says to a foe, "You give me any trouble and I'll fill you full of lead," the words do indeed seem a macabre parody.

To some extent, this sense of doom numbs the movie, despite Walsh's workmanlike efficiency at keeping it going. He has other problems, though. His unsubtle way with actors and perhaps a myopic casting director result in a poor performance from Joan Leslie, who was more at home in sunny musicals than gutsy melodrama. But the film does nothing but benefit from the presence of Bogart, who conveys the sense of futility in Roy Earle without making him pitiful. Critic Manny Farber, an auteurist of sorts who celebrates the work of Walsh, Hawks, and other no-nonsense directors, cites what he calls the "forlorn excitement" of Walsh films as one of their most penetrating qualities. He marvels at Bogie's Roy Earle as a free agent in a world that demands commitments. Indeed, the Bogart figure in the film, though clearly an anachronism, is never quite defeated, even when all the odds are thoroughly against him. "If they get me I haven't got a chance," he tells Marie, "but they ain't gonna get me."

And they don't really. When Roy Earle finally comes down off that mountain, it's because he has sensed the presence of the loyal Marie, has come out of safety to call to her, and is then hit from behind by a hired sniper. The last reels of the film, which include a splendid car chase up mountain roads, build to a stringent climax. Earle has been holed up for hours at the near-top of the mountain while, below, the law tries to get him to surrender and a radio reporter gushes to his listeners: "One is awe-stricken by the gruesomeness of this rendezvous with death." Earle falls almost King Kong-like when finally shot, and when Marie comes upon his dead body on the ground, she asks a newsman what Earle had meant when he'd been talking about "crashing out" to her. "Crashing out means you're free," says the newsman (as in "crash out" of prison). Marie is exhilarated by the sound of the word. "Free!" she says, walking into the camera at fade out. "Free!"

It is the kind of victorious defeat which has awaited other gangsters, whom films often made begrudgingly loveable. In HIGH SIERRA, Roy Earle is a decent, love-needing man who also happens to be a crook. No, not a crook: a criminal. There's a difference. Crooks cheat; criminals steal. When newspapers brand Earle a "Mad Dog," we feel as outraged as he does; we've seen him be kind to a puppy and a cripple, and we have learned he is a hard man with a soft heart.

Somewhere between the adulation of the auteurists and the scorn of their opponents lies a true estimation of the work of Raoul Walsh and other action directors. Pioneer auteurist Andrew Sarris used HIGH SIERRA to help validate a point about the joys of auteurism in a 1962 essay. He called Walsh "one of the screen's most virile directors" who nevertheless acknowledged "the emotional vulnerability of his heroes." The argument prompted a counter-essay from Pauline Kael, who found HIGH SIERRA "not a very good movie" and poo-poo'd much of the auteurist credo.

Walsh made his movies for neither auteurists nor critics, however, and therein lies much of their success. Beyond what they may signify and represent, consciously or subconsciously, they succeed emphatically as popular art, and that "forlorn excitement" survives the ordeal of time.

Hooray for Providence, Wilkes-Barre, Saranac Lake— and Hollywood

Kathleen Karr

"Caribou Bill" Cooper, founder of The Artic Film Company.

As film history had it, Providence, Rhode Island, never became known as the entertainment capital of the world. Yet, films from the mid-teens, recently rediscovered, prove that the motion picture was in motion in various parts of the country, not just where the oranges grow. And, in addition to their status in film history, these films are now records of places and times in Americana that might otherwise be irretrievable.

Prior to the ultimate arrival of Hollywood as "the" American film center in the mid-teens, motion picture companies worked all over the country, in the least expected places. Chicago, Philadelphia, and Fort Lee, New Jersey, were all early contenders for the center of the movie business with the Essanay, Selig, Lubin, Pathé, Solax and other movie studios in residence, but so were Providence, Rhode Island; Wilkes-Barre, Pennsylvania; and Saranac Lake, New York; among dozens of other locales.

Eager to capitalize on the obviously money-making proposition that was capturing the nickels and dimes of America, hordes of small-time entrepreneurs rose out of their holes in the ground to establish local film companies. There were the fly-by-night firms—those run by gentlemen of dubious character on the medicine-show principle: move into a small town with only a camera, convince the inhabitants that they could become stars or buy into the new company for a small fee, then literally run out of town with the funds and the "movie company." It is, however, the legitimate, if less successful, small movie companies which established themselves in provincial America during the first two decades of the century that remain little known, yet offer a revealing picture of the trials and tribulations of the young industry.

A developing interest in location-shooting seems to have been the genesis for most of these firms, but the movement went beyond this stage when well-endowed studios with room for multiple sets, as well as editing and developing facilities, were established.

Possibilities for location shooting were the inspiration for The Arctic Film Company, organized by a traveler of the northern climes, "Caribou Bill" Cooper, around 1909 at Saranac Lake, New York. Cooper built

104

The Vitagraph Company enacts an Indian scalping party in action in one of their films made on the edge of Lake Saranac (1911).

The Arctic Film Company's outdoor studio in Saranac Lake, N.Y. The building in the center was the main stage. A system of pulleys, operated from the three poles to the right, raised or lowered the roof and muslin cover to allow the proper amounts of light to enter the interior set.

a little log cabin village and primitive one-room log cabin stage with Black Maria-like abilities (patterned after Edison's first studio, a series of ropes and pulleys maneuvered the one muslin wall to let in proper amounts of light). He rented these facilities, along with his team of Alaskan huskies, to companies of actors from the Republic Motion Picture Company, Vitagraph, and Lubin for northern-subject photoplays during the snow season, for James Fenimore Cooper stories during the lush summer months, and in off-seasons produced his own films. The movies made at the Cooper camp seem to have long since disappeared, but The American Film Institute has acquired a marvelous collection of still photographs which document the work of the camp and its inhabitants over a four-year period.

There were dozens of other attempts at establishing off-the-beaten-track film companies, from the Prudential Film Corporation of Worcester, Massachusetts; to the western company of Méliès Star Films which operated out of San Antonio, Texas, between 1909 and 1911; to the Japanese-American Film Company which made films for the ethnic market in California in 1914; to the United States Motion Picture Corporation of Wilkes-Barre, Pennsylvania, which made "Rainbow Comedies" for three years on the banks of the Susquehanna; to the Ogden Film Company of Ogden, Utah. Unfortunately, little documentation and fewer films exist from these varied efforts. Research about film companies in New England—another of the unexpected areas of early regional filmmaking—has begun. The occasional films made on Martha's Vineyard (ANNABEL LEE, 1921) and in Maine (TIMOTHY'S QUEST, 1922, produced by a local company, Dirigo Films) have been located and preserved. But the real filming action was to be found in Rhode Island.

In search of good locations close to both the sea and rocky hill country, Essanay director Joseph Byron Totten took his company of actors (including Beverly Bayne) out to his recently purchased farm near Westerly, Rhode Island, in the summer of 1915. Working in and around a Revolutionary War farmhouse several miles from the ocean, Totten and his company found the experience so refreshing that they continued to return until Essanay went out of business. Totten then

A rare shot of auto racing at the old Narragansett Park Asphalt Speedway in Cranston, in a scene from the Eastern Film Corporation's feature film, THE MINISTER, made in Providence, R.I., and environs in 1915.

Cameraman Arnold of the Republic Motion Picture
Company and his wife at "Caribou Bill" Cooper's
Saranac Lake camp.

came back with actors each summer until 1924, following his Essanay experience with affiliations with Vitagraph, and finally, with his own "Tri-Star," "J. B. Totten and Co.," and "Totten-Made" brands. One film survives from the Totten Westerly experience: a two-reel dramatization of an O. Henry story, *The Church with an Overshot Wheel*, made for Vitagraph. Technically, the film is not very interesting, but it becomes important, as do so many of the films made by regional companies, because it incorporates excellent period location shots of the Rhode Island and Connecticut countryside. Fine colonial and Victorian homes and gristmills which no longer stand, as well as the use of the local country people as "extras," remain on record and help to reconstruct part of the American past.

Other filmmaking ventures were tried in Rhode Island, probably the most impressive of which was the Eastern Film Corporation. Inspired by Elwood F. Bostwick, a fast-talking director who came through the backwater areas of Rhode Island in late 1914 shooting at small factory-town locations, Fred Peck, a well-known Rhode Island politician, decided to diversify some of his monies by setting up a studio in Providence. Investing over $300,000 into an old brewery in the spring of 1915, Peck established one of the most elaborate movie studios outside of New York, Chicago, and Hollywood. Bostwick was hired to manage the Eastern studio, and soon a flow of talent was imported from studios all over the United States and Europe. George Lessey and Lambert Hillyer (later the director of many of William S. Hart's films) were among the directors hired, and such old-time actors as Dan Mason and George Bunny (the brother of John Bunny and a comedian in his own right) were raided from the corps of Edison and Biograph. The experiment was a short-lived one, however; production was stopped in the fall of 1915 due primarily to the mishandling of company funds. The actors were sent to winter and produce films in Jacksonville, Florida, under the "Jaxon" trademark, while the posh studio continued to be rented to production firms working out of New York until it was partially destroyed by a fire in the summer of 1917.

Two features (both directed by Lessey) and several shorts survive from the Eastern Film Corporation. Of the features, PARTNERS OF THE TIDE is an action-filled sea story based on a novel by the then-popular Cape Cod writer, Joseph C. Lincoln. THE MINISTER, suggested by Goldsmith's *The Vicar of Wakefield,* is a "modern" morality tale. Both features incorporate the Rhode Island countryside in their location scenes, and much of this footage is priceless today, again because it is the only existing historical material of its kind.

The historical value of their films aside, these small regional companies can be viewed as microcosms of the movie-making methods and problems of the industry as a whole. In addition, research into such enterprises gives a vivid picture of actors and artists trying to work within small-town locations and mentalities at a time when "picture people" were regarded as outcasts of society. One of the surviving actresses of the Eastern Film Corporation recalled the prevailing "civilian" attitude of 1915 with these words, "People from the city and the surrounding towns used to drive out to watch us shoot every Saturday. They were curious to see what *immoral* actors were like. . . . We were freaks."

The cast of the Republic Motion Picture Company enacting a dramatic scene from one of their films made at Cooper's Saranac Lake camp (1912).

Kevin Brownlow

STARK LOVE

Paramount Famous Lasky Corp. 1927.
Producer-Director-Writer: Karl Brown.
Adaptation: Walter Woods.
Cast: Helen Munday, Forrest James, Silas Miracle, Reb Grogan.

There are as many different approaches to truth in film as there are directors. One of the most painstaking efforts is represented by Karl Brown's STARK LOVE, made with great difficulty in 1927. Brown attempted to create a piece of documentary fiction, setting a fanciful narrative against an actual background. The film itself and the tribulations that went into making it say something about the way the camera translates life and the way American agrarians of the twenties—and people generally—looked upon that provocative invention, The Movies.

The film is set in the mountains of North Carolina, among "a primitive people without culture, without civilization but with a law—man is the absolute ruler, woman the slave." Among the people of Wolf Trap Creek, a young man called Rob Warwick has learned how to read. His books open up a new world. He longs to leave his family and go to school in the town.

Rob's closest friend is Barbara Allen (Helen Munday), a young neighbor. Far from here, he tells her, are men who work *and* take care of their women. They are polite and kind and protective. "Would you like that?" he asks.

"No," she replies. "I'm a woman. I can protect myself."

But Rob's enthusiasm is infectious, and Barbara begins to dream of going away with him.

Once a year, the mountaineers assemble for the "funeral feast," which is celebrated for generations of past dead. If on this day the circuit preacher should come, all "wild marriages" are legalized.

This year, the preacher comes. Rob asks the preacher to take him back to town with him. And he makes a momentous decision; he will sell his horse and use the money for the school, but he will pay tuition for Barbara and not himself.

"You shouldn't have taught me all them beautiful things," says Barbara. "Now I'm a longin' for things that won't never be."

Rob goes away. A few days later his ailing and overworked mother dies. His father, Jason Warwick (Silas Miracle), cannot cope without a woman. Barbara goes over to help and finds his house in complete disorder. She takes over, cleans the place out, puts the children to bed, and so impresses Jason that he decides to marry her.

Barbara's father thinks Jason ought to wait while he thinks it over.

"I can't wait. The river's flooding, and if I don't take Barbara now I'll be cut off from you. When the preacher comes again we'll be properly married. What do you say?"

The two men shake hands, but when Barbara hears of it she turns on Jason like a spitfire. It is all he can do to control her.

"You're mighty standoffish," he says finally. "I ain't so bad as I look."

Rob returns from the town, eager to find Barbara. A neighbor tells him the sad news about his mother. Jason returns with Barbara and sees Rob slumped on the floor of the cabin. "Hello, Rob," he says. "Here's your new maw."

An argument breaks out which develops into a furious fight between the two men. Jason calms his son down by banging him violently against the door.

"I don't want to hurt ye, but leave my wife alone!"

Jason hits him in the stomach, and Rob, winded, sinks to the floor. Barbara watches, horrified, from a corner. Rob grabs a rifle. Jason knocks it from his hands, and it falls on the open fire. "Look out!" screams Barbara. The barrel is pointing into the room. The gun goes off, but the bullet misses both men. Jason thrashes Rob and throws him outside. He collapses half in, half out of the rapidly flooding river. Barbara picks up an axe and wields it with ferocious vigor. Jason cringes as she smashes the bolt on the door and races out to rescue Rob. The river, swollen and angry, carries them both away. Fighting desperately, Barbara manages to bring Rob to shore downstream.

Morning sees the start of a new life; Rob and Barbara set out together to cross the mountains.

* * *

This simple story provides the basis for one of the most fascinating and unusual films ever made in America. Karl Brown's decision to make the whole thing on location meant the difference between just

110

another melodrama and a work of art. Virtually every member of the cast is a real mountaineer. There is no make-up; the quality of the faces, the texture of the rough skin is carefully and affectionately captured by the camera, and the effect is reminiscent of 17th Century Dutch painting. The compositions crystallize the atmosphere but are never obtrusive.

Every new scene carries the pleasure of discovery. Brown tells us exactly what we want to know; he explains the origins of the settlers, he illustrates the way they live, their manner of dress, and their customs and traditions. He shows how, when they die, their bodies are placed in miniature cabins as protection from the wolves. He shows us women skinning an animal in the one room of the cabin, while the men sit around, drinking moonshine. But none of this is presented dryly, in the manner of most factual films. Every facet of mountain life is a legitimate part of the story. STARK LOVE stands as a priceless record of a primitive way of life which, while it still exists, requires the courage of a Karl Brown to investigate.

STARK LOVE was Karl Brown's first film as a director. He had been G. W. Bitzer's assistant on THE BIRTH OF A NATION and INTOLERANCE, and had operated second camera on both productions. He worked with the Griffith company from 1913 right through to BROKEN BLOSSOMS, when Griffith left for Mamaroneck, New York. Brown then joined Famous Players-Lasky, and worked for James Cruze as first cameraman. His most celebrated achievement was the photography for THE COVERED WAGON.

After STARK LOVE, and a picture for the De Mille organization, Karl Brown became a prolific screenwriter. He later wrote and directed for Monogram, and wrote for television. Upon his retirement he determined to settle into obscurity. He was therefore extremely difficult to trace. Once discovered, however, Mr. Brown proved to be a gold mine of information. After many interviews, he finally agreed to write a book about his career. The first volume, on his days with Griffith, is an amazingly eloquent and exciting book—which will be published in 1973.

The idea for STARK LOVE developed from the big outdoor pictures, such as THE COVERED WAGON and PONY EXPRESS. "I noticed," said Brown, "that

the Indians and the local people were better than our Hollywood actors when it came to professionalism."

The problem, even in that enlightened era, was one of backing. Brown was employed by Famous Players-Lasky (Paramount) and was one of their best cameramen. The chance of his being released to direct a film was slender. Then NANOOK OF THE NORTH, by Flaherty, and GRASS, by Cooper and Schoedsack, encouraged a new attitude toward naturalistic pictures. In 1926, Jesse Lasky financed MOANA by Flaherty and CHANG by Cooper and Schoedsack. Brown had to wait three years, but at last Lasky gave him the go-ahead.

"We may lose money," he said. "But go down to North Carolina and find out whether it's feasible to make such a picture."

Brown's pre-production trip was hair-raising. There were only 5,000 mountaineers left and it proved hard to locate them. He wandered round the Great Smoky Mountains with one companion, his assistant director, an ex-regular Army man called Captain Paul Wing. Trails were few, and they even had to blast their way through certain areas. It took them fifteen days to go 200 miles.

"To make contact with the mountain people," Brown said, "I first of all went to Horace Kephart, a friend in the East who was quite famous in his day—there was a mountain named for him. He told me what not to do, but he wouldn't tell me what to do. He simply illustrated a thing I'd known a long time and has yet to fail me; that if you go into any country—that is, if you're not at war—and behave yourself as a gentleman should, nobody will ever bother you. Mind your own business, keep out of other people's trouble, don't interfere with anything, just do what you're supposed to do. That's the way with the mountain people. They're naturally suspicious and so you just go about your business until they observe, or by some sort of psychic osmosis, learn that you are not up to any harm, you're not going to turn them in, you really are going to do what you're supposed to do, From that point on, everything is plain sailing.

"I had discovered, quite some time before this, that the easiest actors to handle are children. They

Forrest James and Helen Munday in STARK LOVE.

are naturally imitative, that's how they learn. Now if you try to tell anybody, even a pretty good actor, how to do something, he'll unconsciously resent it. He feels that he knows his business. And so I had learned, mostly from watching Griffith do the same thing, and later on Cruze—never tell an actor what to do. Tell him what is to be done.

"Helen Munday was the most difficult person I ever had anything to do with. Wing found her; she came from Knoxville. I found a girl who was much better than Munday. She lived on the mountain and was everything she was supposed to be. But when it came to getting parental consent, her hillbilly father said, 'I'd see her dead an' in her coffin before I see her play-actin' for nobody.' So Wing disappeared and came back bringing Helen Munday in tow.

"I was so desperate at the time that I didn't ask too many questions. I took her out and made some still pictures of her, and a few tests, shot them back to New York and they practically burned up, saying, 'How did you ever find her down there?' But the famous ones, like Pola Negri, were nothing compared to this one. She learned very early in the game that she was the only girl in the picture, that without her the picture could not be made, and so it was virtually a case of blackmail. 'Give me this' or 'Get me that—or I'm gone.'

"So she went. The others said, 'Well, there goes your picture.'

"'Maybe it does,' I said, 'but I'm not going to make a picture at the cost of all this.' About two hours later she came creeping back. Her bluff hadn't worked.

"Wing and I were having dinner in Knoxville one night and about three tables away were four boys, laughing and having a fine time. The one farthest from me was exactly the type that I had in mind for the boy. I said, 'We should try to meet that fellow.'

"Wing just got a waiter over, wrote a note, and said, 'Give it to that gentleman over there.' He read it and came over, and I let Wing do the talking. Yes, he was willing to do it. He was part of a football team and they had just won something somewhere and they were celebrating. So we took him in and he made the picture. He was very silent. He would sulk in his tent like Achilles. He had very little to say to anybody. But he got through with his part and as soon as he got through it he was gone. Nobody ever heard of him again.

"Everyone else in the picture were real mountain people."

*   *   *

"We discovered a rocky outcrop that would block any sort of wagon road. We had to get our supplies in and out, so we decided to blast it out. They were building a dam on the river forty or fifty miles away, so we had a ready supply of dynamite and experienced men to use it. We simply blasted that ridge away.

"Instead of shooting the interiors in a studio, we used an actual cabin and took two walls out—so we could get cross shots. Part of the roof remained in place. We used reflectors for daylight shots, and for night shots, with the firelight showing, I used special acetylene lights.

"For the river scenes, we had to create our own flood. We built a dam upstream with a break away arrangement. When the water got up to six or eight feet we could blow up one end of it and the whole river would rush on down.

"One connecting shot was made in the studio at Astoria. I not only did not want, I did not *like*, any part of the water sequence that ends the picture at the present time. To me, that was just a cheap melodramatic trick that was completely out of key with the picture. Once the girl moved out and joined the boy and started to walk down the mountain, that's the end of the story. You don't have to do anything else, but New York insisted. And so I had to go back and shoot that water stuff later, and we needed a connecting shot to get the thing to flow through. So we took it in one long shot at Astoria—they duplicated the interior from stills, duplicated the costumes and stuck on beards and that was it. But it was a whole day's work for one scene.

"We had no rushes on location. Everything was blind. We took the standard amount of stills, but we never showed them to the mountain people. They had a complete lack of interest. They had no curiosity, no understanding. They just didn't care, that was all there was to it. It was no use explaining anything, they thought you were crazy anyway. We were paying such enormous salaries—everyone got twenty-five dollars a week, leading man, leading woman, everyone. That way there could be no quarrels, no jealousy.

"Walter Woods thought up the title STARK LOVE. I didn't particularly like it, but nobody came up with a better one, so we let it go. When it was released it did pretty well in America—I understand it did very well indeed in Europe. I say pretty well—it ran about two or three weeks. Ordinarily, a picture would run a week. But it wasn't one of those things like THE COVERED WAGON or THE BIRTH OF A NATION that run for a year. It also had the handicap of being the first of its kind. It was a stranger in town—nobody knew quite what to make of it. I don't want to take too much credit upon myself, because Bob Flaherty had already made NANOOK OF THE NORTH, but that was a straight document—no attempt was made to tell a story.

"As a matter of fact, STARK LOVE was such a maverick in design, conception, and everything else that nobody in the sales department knew what to do with it. And there was considerable talk about simply shelving it. It didn't cost much and it wouldn't be much of a loss. So that was that. But they did put it out and everybody was astonished—including myself."

Frank Capra

Tom Shales

*If movies are the populist art, Frank Capra is one of
the greatest of populist artists. He made his pictures
not for awards committees or critics but for the people
who bought the tickets—the people, period, as he
himself might say. What they often saw was the
common-sense triumph of a common man, a theme
they were bound to appreciate, and a moral always
put over with style and vigor. Frank Capra's films,
are not only the* oeuvre *of one dynamic director but
also a significant part of the national literature. They
tell us almost as much about America as about Capra.*

Walter Huston quelling the bank run in AMERICAN MADNESS,
1932.

Frank Capra has made so many movies about American heroes that he has become an American hero himself. Certainly American, and definitely heroic. His is
the essence of the grass-roots success story—the poor
immigrant who grows up to be rich and famous, taking a lot of hard knocks along the way, fiercely and
even ferociously individualistic, believing in the basic
meat-and-potatoes values and knowing that scoundrels
and rascals can be defeated if one has honesty, integ-
rity, and, when necessary, a good left hook.

In Frank Capra's films, good men suffer but eventually win out—be they just-folks, tuba-playing Mr.
Deeds, or just-folks, ecology-loving Mr. Smith. For
some, the doses of romanticism and optimism proved
too strong. One critic has invented the term "Frank
Capracorn" to use for works that may see too much
unwarranted hope. But Capra must at least be given
credit, even from his detractors, for the consistency
of his vision. It is a sincere set of beliefs, not a contrived commercial code designed to lure customers.
They're lured all right, but it's because they recognize and perhaps share the Capra values—and also
because they like good stories told well.

Capra likes to talk about his films and why he
made them. He goes on at some length in his rough-
and-ready autobiography, *The Name Above the Title*
(MacMillan, 1971). During a discussion at The American Film Institute's Center for Advanced Film Studies
on May 26, 1971, he defended his common-man obsession and said it grew out of "my own youth, things
that were involved with that. There was the fact that

Loretta Young, Robert Williams, and Jean Harlow in PLATINUM BLONDE, 1931.

Ronald Colman, Isabel Jewell, and Thomas Mitchell in LOST HORIZON, 1937.

Gary Cooper and Jean Arthur in MR. DEEDS GOES TO TOWN, 1936.

Frank Capra is well represented in the AFI Collection; his films are part of the extensive Columbia Pictures collection. Capra worked at Columbia with that mythical monster, Harry Cohn. He may have been one of the few people who could get his way with Cohn and make pictures the way he wanted them made.

One of the earliest films by Capra in the Collection is his melodrama THE YOUNGER GENERATION (1929), which he describes in his autobiography as the story of "a social-climbing super-Jew who denied his parents." The film is not typical Capra, but it does reflect his prowess in developing and animating a narrative—in this case, a pretty maudlin one. It was adapted from a Fannie Hurst play, "It Is to Laugh," by Columbia's Sonya Levien. The cast was a good one and included actor Jean Hersholt as the denied father.

The film has value as a transitional oddity as well because it was made during the earliest infant squeals of Hollywood sound. Capra shot the film half-sound and half-silent so that he would be prepared in either eventuality: if the talkies were a fad, or the waves of the future. Shooting sound when he was used to silent was "an etude of chaos," he writes, but the film, though certainly awkward, doesn't suffer as much as it ought to under this sporadic approach—one reel sound, the next two silent, the next one sound, and so on.

THE YOUNGER GENERATION tells of the Goldfish family, poor Jews living on the lower East Side of New York. Papa likes to stand and talk to his friends during the day; Mama wants him to get rich. Giving up on him, she turns to her son Morris and rears him to be a good little capitalist. Papa protests with a line that sounds symptomatically Capran: "Money ain't good for nothing, Mama—if it don't buy happiness." As usual, it doesn't.

Morris grows up to be Heel No. 1 of all time. He throws his sister out into the cold because "You've disgraced me in the business world and ruined me socially!" Later he will deny that his mother and father are his parents, pretending they are servants for the benefit of rich snob friends who are laughing at the pathetic old couple. Soon after that, Papa dies.

I had always been a rebel, against conformity; for the individual, against mass conformity. That means mass conformity of any kind. I see mass conformity happening again today, and I just don't like it . . . I'd rather see some individuals. That was the common-man idea. I didn't think he was common; I thought he was a hell of a guy. I thought he was the hope of the world."

Frank Capra directing.

Money has not only failed to buy happiness, it has bought more unhappiness than anybody deserves. At the end of the film, Morris the cad is left alone in his big cold apartment. The venetian blinds make a prison-like shadow on the wall. As in many Capra films to come, the middle-class audience could take assurance from further evidence that the rich are miserable. Papa was happier when he was poor.

Capra's talkie comedy PLATINUM BLONDE (1931) continued the message that money corrupts but said it much more snappily. Capra says the story was "stolen" from THE FRONT PAGE (1931), though there aren't really many similarities. The dialogue is by Robert Riskin, who would write many of Capra's best films: "We both seemed to vibrate to the same tuning fork," said Capra of Riskin at the AFI. In PLATINUM BLONDE, a tough-living newspaper reporter marries a rich society dame and finds out that the soft life isn't for him. He goes back to his old job and to the girl who has loved him madly throughout the whole picture—it was obvious to everybody but him, of course.

The picture has great sparkle and the Capra flair. It benefits from the presence of Jean Harlow, one of the few actresses who could be sexy even while being funny, and Robert Williams, a singular comic actor. Loretta Young in her flapper hat makes a most appealing girl-who-waits.

As a Capra hero, the reporter fits most of the qualifications. When we first meet him, he is supposed to be working but prefers instead to diddle with a puzzle—Capra gave his heroes idiosyncrasies that were to symbolize their individuality and lack of concern over doing the "right" thing. They didn't care what banks failed in Yonkers or anywhere else, really. Many aspects of the reporter's personality would be repeated in the hero of MR. DEEDS GOES TO TOWN (1936) as well as in Clark Gable's reporter in IT HAPPENED ONE NIGHT (1934). Like Mr. Deeds, the reporter becomes known as "The Cinderella Man" because he has come into money suddenly—even though he is not especially impressed by the fortune. Like Mr. Deeds, he believes firmly in the efficacy of a belt in the mouth—like Deeds, he socks a lawyer (lawyers and big businessmen were fair game in Capra movies) and

also hits a fellow reporter. The hero's observation of a butler's "puttering" is not unlike the "doodling" that Mr. Deeds notices while he's on trial for allegedly being insane. And one sequence from BLONDE appears again in DEEDS with few changes—the one in which the reporter stands in the hallway of a big rich house and teaches the servants how to make an echo in the marble halls. Again, the Capra hero functions true to form—elegance and pomposity are balloons to be punctured. They are phony and unnecessary. We are happier without them.

PLATINUM BLONDE doesn't work as well as later Capra films. After long prefatory scenes, the premise is set up, a bit late, in a short expository dialogue between Harlow and another character. It's too abrupt and perfunctory. And the reporter's slugging instinct becomes tiresome. It gets ludicrous when he even threatens his foolishly loyal girl-back-home: "I should sock you right in that funny little nose." The moral of the film is obvious, but the reporter announces it anyway when he leaves Harlow on his way back to the simple life. "I know I'm out of my crowd," he says. "I'll stay in my own back yard from now on." (It was a common theme in the thirties—culminating, perhaps, in Dorothy's promise to Aunt Em never to run away again in THE WIZARD OF OZ. Know your place, and stay there.)

It would not be fair to say that the rich were universally villainous in the Capra films. If they could behave like regular people, they got approval. In his film AMERICAN MADNESS (1932), Capra celebrates a bank president who hasn't forgotten the little folk who put him in authority. Likewise, they do not forget him. They come marching to his rescue when the bank is failing and the sneaky board of directors is clamoring for the president's resignation. In his autobiography, Capra calls this his first realistic, non-escapist film. It dealt with the realities of Depression America. Of course, it did not deal with them in the most harshly realistic of terms. It saw a light at the end of the tunnel; it saw hope so long as people kept their heads and didn't panic.

Its hero was ably embodied in Walter Huston, who is faced with crises at every turn in his business and personal life. But he trusts people, contrary to the

Clark Gable and Claudette Colbert in IT HAPPENED ONE NIGHT, 1934.

wishes of the board of directors; and they return that trust with loyalty and faith. When they make their last ditch, nickles-and-dimes effort to save the bank, it is a gesture similar to that made by all those good little boys who put out their own newspaper to see that their champion gets a fair shake in MR. SMITH GOES TO WASHINGTON (1939). And the diligence pays off for both men. They win because right is on their side. Gee whiz.

"If my films . . . smack here and there of gee whiz," writes Capra, "well, 'Gee whiz!' To some of us, all that meets the eye *is* larger than life, including life itself. Who can match the wonder of it? . . . We, the gee-whizzers, euphemistically say we are of the 'upbeat' school, in contrast to the 'down-beaters' whom we non-euphemistically relegate to the 'ashcan' school, because their films depict life as an alley of cats clawing lids off garbage cans, and man as less noble than a hyena."

Besides again exemplifying the Capra ethic, AMERICAN MADNESS reflects the increased Capra tempo. The film rushes along with a dynamism new to his films—a quality that would certainly remain. At the AFI, he explained how he achieved the brisk effect he wanted: "In AMERICAN MADNESS, for the first time, I purposefully speeded up the shooting of every scene by about 40 percent above normal. Not with the camera but actually with the actors. . . . I just upped the pace. . . . I did that in practically all of the pictures I made, except for mood scenes where pace was not a factor. But in normal scenes, I shot them about 40 percent faster than normal and then they seemed to be normal on the screen. . . . There was an urgency to the scenes that seemed to work."

MADNESS moves. It shows a new visual awareness by Capra, too. There are such nice touches as the short pan along a glissando on the piano which continues to a man seated at the right of the piano when two characters enter a room and find him there. The visual and musical motions are neatly synchronized. To demonstrate how a single rumor can be blown out of proportion—how, in fact, fear spreads through a community—Capra devised a hectic telephone montage, a geometric progression from one blabby switchboard operator. At the end of the film, Capra skill-

fully keeps several lines of action rushing toward a climax at once: the bank president is faced with the prospect of a cheating wife; the cops are interrogating an innocent man as a hold-up suspect; the innocent man can't confess because that would reveal the bank president's wife to be unfaithful; other cops meanwhile are chasing the real crook; the customers downstairs are making a mad run on the bank, and the tellers are running low on cash; the board of directors is haggling in another room and trying to get rid of the president so they can take over the bank and be unscrupulous; and the bank president is desperately trying to raise money to save the bank and preserve the faith of his friends who've entrusted him with their life savings. Somehow, it all works out happily. And quickly.

The team was definitely Riskin and Capra now, and they worked together again, perhaps to their greatest philosophical success, on MR. DEEDS GOES TO TOWN, in 1936. Gary Cooper wore the mantle of the Capra hero this time as the bashful, peaceful (except when antagonized), music-loving, poetry-writing Mr. Deeds, who comes to evil New York and lets himself be made a fool of, somehow emerging triumphant in the end—putting down the haughty and the sophisticated as only a Capra hero can.

Mr. Deeds is living happily in Mandrake Falls, Vermont, when big city lawyers arrive to tell him he has inherited twenty million dollars from a dead uncle. "I wonder why he left me all that money," says Mr. Deeds. "I don't need it." The most sinister of the lawyers, played by the ever-sinister Douglas Dumbrille, is delighted to find Mr. Deeds such a yokel. "We've nothing to worry about," he tells his partners. "He's naive as a child."

Naive, yes, but not a fool. The sweet old housekeeper, the Dalmatian, the little bow tie, and the tuba that help make up his life style do not hide the fact— from us—that he is more than a bumpkin. He is a poet—though his poetry is terrible—a loner, a nonconformist, and a devout non-materialist. For him, the best things in life are free indeed. They are the everyday pleasures of smalltown America.

In New York, Mr. Deeds is ridiculed by the press, but we see him taking the stuffings out of many stuffed shirts. He dispenses with the sissies—Franklin Pangborn, as a tailor, is discharged. He liberates his valet: "Don't ever get on your knees to me." He escapes constraints—locking his bodyguards in the closet. He eschews sophistication—sliding down the banister in his mansion. He banishes high society snobs—"I threw 'em out." He stands up to the literati —starting a fistfight at a writers' hangout when they make fun of his poems. False stateliness and pretentiousness are crumbled—he interrupts a meeting of the opera society's board of directors to rush to a window shouting, "Hey, there's a fire engine!"

"In quiet places," wrote Adlai Stevenson, "reason abounds." Mr. Deeds represents that same faith in common-man, small-town, good-neighbor America. Mr. Deeds is the modern-day incarnation of the pioneer spirit; he is the church supper, the old hand pump, the freshly baked apple pie on the windowsill. Mr. Deeds may be the most profound and convincing of all the heroes Capra unleashed on a needy world. "People here are funny," Deeds says when he gets to New York. "They work so hard at living they forget how to live."

Obviously, the Capra-Riskin formula might not always work. It could easily be picked apart. But *how* it was said was as important as what it was saying.

And it was said very well indeed. It was made fast and funny and alert to the rhythms of the people out there. Capra always had the audience in mind. His films were carefully tested before preview crowds. When they didn't respond to something, out it went. The story of how he burned the first two reels of LOST HORIZON (1937) in order to save the picture has become a legend, true as it is. The individualism he espoused in his films he also practiced when making them. "I don't like anybody telling me what to do," he said at the AFI. "If you took it all on yourself—it's poor, but it's my own—you could take it. That's the way pictures should be made: one man, one film."

His autobiography begins with his movie credo: "There are no rules in filmmaking, only sins. And the cardinal sin is Dullness." Whatever his other sins, he scarcely ever committed that one. He knew the secret of his own success and explained it at the AFI:

"I told a form of human comedy. I dealt with serious problems, protest films, but they were done with entertainment. They were done primarily through comedy. That's a very tough thing to do—doesn't always come off. But I was able to make that come off, and that was why they were entertaining."

HERE COMES MR. JORDAN:
From Script to Screen

Bruce Henstell

Columbia Pictures. 1941.
Director: Alexander Hall.
Screenplay: Sidney Buchman and Seton I. Miller, based on a play by Harry Segall.
Cast: Robert Montgomery, Evelyn Keyes, Claude Rains, Rita Johnson, Edward Everett Horton.

Robert Montgomery in HERE COMES MR. JORDAN.

"There is only one event in making movies," said Arthur Penn in an interview, "and that's the director's event. It's not anybody else's." Penn, of course, is a director. But without the script, there would be nothing to direct. In the days of the omnipotent studios, a director was probably more dependent on his script than is today's auteur-era director, and Hollywood lured some of the most formidable writing talent in America during the thirties and forties. The story of HERE COMES MR. JORDAN is the odyssey of an idea, from conception to script to fruition on film.

When the Academy Awards were given out for 1941, HERE COMES MR. JORDAN took the kudos for writing: Harry Segall received the award for best original story, and Sidney Buchman and Seton I. Miller the award for the best written screenplay. The film was a popular success, establishing a minor genre of gentle comedies about death. The audience's acceptance of the unusual theme of the film owed almost all to the excellent screenplay. Therefore, HERE COMES MR. JORDAN is a good choice from The American Film Institute Collection for exploring the writing part of the filmmaking process.

The story was originally written as a play entitled "It Was Like This" by Harry Segall. Segall, of Chicago newspaper background, had been a contract writer at RKO. His credits include: FATAL LADY (Paramount), SUPER-SLEUTH (RKO), and DON'T TURN 'EM LOOSE (RKO). "It Was Like This" was written while Segall was in New York, and was submitted to Columbia. There it came to the attention of Sam Briskin, second in command to Harry Cohn. Briskin liked the property enough to offer Segall a job and pay his way back to Hollywood, but the studio did not purchase the property.

Harry Cohn disliked it, as did Columbia's New York office who felt the public would hardly go to see a film in which death was the hero and reincarnation the theme. Columbia's story editor, the astute D. A. Doran, urged the property so strongly upon Cohn that Cohn finally threatened to throw him off the lot.

Robert Montgomery and Edward Everett Horton in HERE COMES MR. JORDAN.

Meanwhile, in October of 1939, Lewis Milestone and Jed Harris acquired the rights to the property, planning to produce it on Broadway. In July of 1940, Milestone withdrew from the unrealized project and transferred his rights to Harris. During this time "It Was Like This" came to the attention of Everett Riskin.

Riskin was one of that rare breed of film producers whose sharp business sense was matched with deep creative sensitivity. His credits include such exceptional films as: THE AWFUL TRUTH, THE KING STEPS OUT, and THEODORA GOES WILD. Riskin's insistence upon the potentialities of the play convinced Cohn, who trusted the instincts of men such as Riskin. In December of 1940, Columbia acquired the rights to the property.

Production was quick, clean, and efficient. The budget was small: $895,464; and the final cost slightly less: $881,275. By January of 1941, Riskin had hired Seton Miller to prepare the first draft of a screenplay.

Miller, the respected author of films such as THE CRIMINAL CODE and THE DAWN PATROL, worked on a short-term contract dated January 9, 1941. If we take the date of the final typing of his second draft as the time of completion, he finished his work on JORDAN by the end of February. Miller performed two main tasks in writing: he opened up the play, adding scenes only alluded to, and smoothed out the dialogue, reducing the number of gags. The form and language of the play was mostly preserved. The title had now become "Heaven Can Wait."

Most of the writing of JORDAN was done by Sidney Buchman, then one of the top writers under contract at Columbia and the author of the superlative MR. SMITH GOES TO WASHINGTON. Buchman provided the essential smooth quality of the film, adding even more scenes than had Miller, and developing further the relationship between the hero and heroine. But Buchman and Miller at no time consulted in any way about the film. Buchman, in fact, disliked the project and asked Riskin to remove his name even after the successful first previews.

The most crucial scene in the film, the producer and both writers fully realized, was when the prize-fighter hero, mistakenly taken by heaven before his time, is given a new body. The scene was played without make-up or costume changes to make it less showy or dramatic and thus more acceptable to the audience. Miller added this scene and had it take place in the bathroom before a mirror. Buchman added dialogue and the device of opening the scene on the back of the heavenly messenger Jordan as well as cutting to reveal Jordan helping the hero, encased in his new body, into a robe.

By April, writing was concluded, and in May the script went before the cameras. Scheduled at thirty-six days, production was concluded in thirty-eight days. "Heaven Can Wait" had become "Mr. Jordan Comes to Town" and finally HERE COMES MR. JORDAN, the title under which it was released in August of 1941.

Antecedents of CITIZEN KANE *Tom Shales*

Orson Welles is one of the colossus figures of American film history even though his output has been relatively small, for reasons both mysterious and mundane. Whether Welles did or did not "invent" certain techniques—some say, erroneously, that he was the first to shoot interiors with the ceiling showing—is beside the point, and exactly who should get credit for what in Welles' most famous film, CITIZEN KANE, may be in the last analysis irrelevant too. But the apparently endless investigations into the origins and sources of that great work go on, not to detract from the Welles renown but as the logical outcome of fascination with a masterpiece.

It in no way tarnishes the lustre of CITIZEN KANE to say that it was not completely unprecedented. There is precedent, after all, for everything: for the first movie, for the first talkie, and for CITIZEN KANE. The Welles film was startling, original, and complex, and it did so many things in such seemingly untried ways that Bosley Crowther of *The New York Times* exclaimed, "It comes close to being the most sensational film ever made in Hollywood," but nevertheless, it did not burst full-grown from the head of Orson Welles (or his collaborators). It was the result of much that had gone before.

In her landmark essay "Raising Kane," Pauline Kael sees KANE as, among other things, the culmination of the wisecracking satirical comedies of the thirties. Though the film is not a comedy itself, it has a comedy's drive and kinetic tension, and it has snappy-crisp dialogue written by the ultimate newspaperman-turned-screenwriter, Herman J. Mankiewicz. It was, Kael suggests, the logical outcome of the fast-talking comedies on which Mankiewicz and other ex-journalists had made their thirties fortunes.

John Houseman, script editor on the film and an old Welles crony, spent ten weeks with "Mank" working on the script, then called "American." In his recently published autobiography, *Run Through* (Simon & Schuster, 1972), Houseman recalls that first draft in terms that make it sound, indeed, much like the archetypal thirties comedies—"more than 400 pages long—overrich, repetitious, loaded with irrelevant, fas-

Rosebud, the symbol of Kane's childhood in CITIZEN KANE, 1941.

Bill O'Brien and Cullen Johnston in the childhood sequence of THE POWER AND THE GLORY, 1933.

Joseph Cotton, Orson Welles, and Everett Sloane in CITIZEN KANE.

Adolph Menjou, Edward Everett Horton and Pat O'Brien in THE FRONT PAGE, 1931.

Cary Grant and Rosalind Russell in HIS GIRL FRIDAY, 1940.

cinating detail and private jokes, of which we loved every one." Houseman verifies, for the record, Kael's point about Mankiewicz deserving primary credit for the screenplay. He says that Welles mainly consulted on the work-in-motion: "Orson telephoned at odd hours to inquire after our progress. On the appointed day, at the end of six weeks, he arrived in a limousine driven by a dwarf, read a hundred pages of script, discussed our outline of the rest . . . and returned to Los Angeles."

CITIZEN KANE (1941) can be seen as the extension of other trends besides thirties comedy. It was also to some extent the culmination of the "Newspaper Movie." Throughout the thirties, newspaper stories had been immensely popular on the screen, and newspaper reporters were true working-class heroes—and middle-class heroes, too. They were ruthless, smart-alecky, clever, sarcastic, and above all and always, unsentimental. Ordinary mush didn't fool them, and they looked on life's assorted tragedies with skepticism or dispassion. This was true not only in newspaper movies, like THE FRONT PAGE (also in The American Film Institute Collection), but in other comedies, potboilers and thrillers as well. Capra's PLATINUM BLONDE has a tough-talking newshound as its hero, and the same director's MR. DEEDS GOES TO TOWN has Jean Arthur as a hardboiled woman reporter. In THE MYSTERY OF THE WAX MUSEUM, newspaper reporters are behaving typically—according to the movie image—when they surround the body of a dead girl and, on learning that she was a suicide, say seemingly heartless things like, "Boy, what a swell story!" A newspaper reporter's snooping was a key element in such other period thrillers as DR. X; Flash Gordon took along a newspaper reporter named Happy Hapgood on his third (and last) journey into outer space. Reporters made good catalysts for action narratives because they could be counted on to poke into business that was none of theirs, and they knew no fear. Witness the "gentlemen of the press" in KING KONG who, when told their popping flashbulbs are enraging the monster, merely scoff, "Aw, let him roar. It makes a swell picture." There are countless other examples.

Newspaper reporters made, in their own phrase, hot **129**

Orson Welles in CITIZEN KANE.

copy. CITIZEN KANE's screenplay, written by an ex-newspaperman who filled many of the stereotypes in his real life, is hot copy too. It has such vitality that, after thirty years, we can still feel the journalism in it. Essentially it is fictional, or semi-fictional, reportage filmed by a man who was a master of another old art, the theatre.

Originally, the film was not supposed to be about a publishing magnate but about criminal John Dillinger (Houseman told this reporter that the idea of doing Hearst could not be attributed solely to Welles or to Mankiewicz—it was a kind of mutual inspiration). It was not the subject, however, but the style of telling the story that instigated the project. Welles himself discussed it on "The David Frost Show" in June of 1970: "I'll tell you how it started—an idea that was used years later in a Japanese film called RASHO-MON, which is several different people telling a story. You see the same story again from each point of view, and each time it's different.... That was the beginning of KANE, to make such a film with different people.... You would see an entirely different man because somebody else was telling the story." Mankiewicz called it a "prismatic" approach to narrative. But he and Welles were not the first to use the technique. It was employed by another prominent screenwriter, Preston Sturges, in William K. Howard's film, THE POWER AND THE GLORY (1933).

THE POWER AND THE GLORY, which AFI is restoring, is the prismatically told biography of railroad tycoon Thomas Garner. The similarities to KANE as film and as central character are obvious. Like KANE, POWER opens with the death of its hero—Kane drops the glass ball and says "Rosebud," while Garner is already gone, a suicide, and the film of his life opens at his funeral.

One of the mourners at the funeral gets up during the eulogy and walks out. We next see him at the railroad office, where an elevator operator remembers the late Mr. Garner with something less than devotion: "I'm glad he croaked, the old ———." The mourner, Garner's long-time defender, Henry, goes home, where his wife threatens to throw away a portrait of the deceased: "I won't have his picture in my house. It's a good thing he killed himself!" Henry cautions his

Prelude to KANE: Orson Welles in his early experimental film, HEARTS OF AGE, 1934.

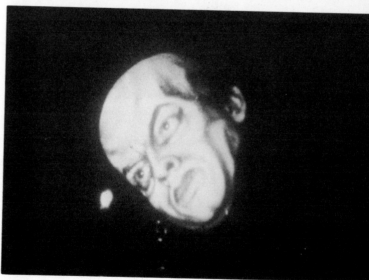

wife: "You can't judge him by ordinary standards. He was too big."

Thus is it established that, like Kane, Garner is a "great man" damned by some and lauded by others. But though the Garner story may be told in a prismatic way, the prism is constructed not with the vigor and daring that went into KANE but instead with

Spencer Tracy and Colleen Moore at the birth of their son, THE POWER AND THE GLORY.

laggardly and sometimes lugubriously old-fashioned flashbacks—not in chronological order, perhaps, but more blatantly "organized" and arranged than the recollections in KANE, which seem to flow spontaneously.

At times, the superficial similarities to KANE in THE POWER AND THE GLORY do seem striking. For the first flashback into the Garner boy's youth, there is a leisurely pan from present-day Henry to a childhood lagoon that, in style, resembles that perfect dissolve in KANE from the words written in a diary to a winter snowfall; young Charlie playing in the yard with his sled while, inside, his mother is signing his life away.

Despite the similarities, deep or surface, POWER differs from KANE most importantly in one crucial aspect: quality. One film is a maudlin melodrama and the other is a masterpiece. POWER never really tells us why those who knew and worked with Garner thought of him as a bastard except for the fact that he jilted his long-loyal wife. He isn't really subject to even a cursory psychological study, as Kane is. Further, the Howard film grows grossly sentimental at times—a tendency Welles thoroughly avoids—in such scenes as the one in which Garner's son is born. While the sound-track orchestra strikes up "Ave Maria," Spencer Tracy, as Garner, gasps, "We've got a son! Thank you, God!" and recites "The Lord's Prayer," giving special emphasis to the phrase, "For Thine is the kingdom and the power and the glory." The flashback ends, and faithful old Henry reflects, "The power and the glory! What they can do to a man!" Besides such lapses, the film is guilty of a structural error that KANE also, to a lesser degree, commits: people recall flashbacks of scenes they never could have witnessed.

There are other films that can be called predecessors of CITIZEN KANE in style or content. Kael lists such newspaper or newspaper-related pictures as FIVE STAR FINAL (1931), BLESSED EVENT (1932), LIBELED LADY (1936), and HIS GIRL FRIDAY with Cary Grant and Rosalind Russell, the 1940 Howard Hawks remake of Hecht and MacArthur's THE FRONT PAGE (1931). Charles Higham, who wrote *The Films of Orson Welles* (University of California Press,

1970), finds similarities to the KANE story in such earlier films as I LOVED A WOMAN (1933) and A MAN TO REMEMBER (1938). He also says that Welles, before shooting began on KANE, immersed himself in the work of such directors as John Ford, Fritz Lang, René Clair, King Vidor, and Frank Capra. Ford's THE INFORMER (1935) "impressed and most deeply influenced him," writes Higham, who goes on to say, "KANE has been called a revolutionary work, but it is in fact a creation in the mainstream of America's film art, a deeply traditionalist reflection of the native cinema's major virtues: energy and forcefulness, physical glamor, and strength of purpose."

CITIZEN KANE was not, even strictly speaking, the first film made by Orson Welles. He had previously done filmed segments for his legendary stage productions with the Mercury Theatre in New York. Welles also made a short, one-reel film (about five minutes) in 1934, HEARTS OF AGE, a 16mm print of which has been uncovered by the AFI through the efforts of the Greenwich (Connecticut) Public Library and placed in the Collection along with the original camera negative of CITIZEN KANE. Little is known about the precise origins of the film. Welles plays the central role, a kind of conjurer, and the film reflects a fascination with death that, says Houseman, Welles has had all his life. HEARTS OF AGE is primarily experimental, and it reveals some of the Welles tricks with camera angles and lighting that would later distinguish KANE.

For all the qualifications that can be made about the alleged originality of Kane—no matter how many films can be cited as having influenced, in some way, its style or substance—the film was still, in many ways, a revolution. If many of its ingredients were already there, if some of its basic elements and keen ideas were derivations from past works and traditions, no one can deny that the way they were assembled and put across was in every sense of the word brilliant—and brilliant in a novel, engaging, almost overwhelming way. As even the avidly debunking Miss Kael must admit, "CITIZEN KANE is perhaps the one American talking picture that seems as fresh now as the day it opened. It may seem even fresher."

Welles himself contemplated the reasons for that freshness in a 1965 interview (reprinted in *Hollywood Voices*, Bobbs-Merrill, 1971, edited by Andrew Sarris): "I had . . . the good fortune to have Gregg Toland, who is the best director of photography that ever existed, and I also had the luck to hit upon actors who had never worked in films before; not a single one of them had ever found himself in front of a camera until then. They all came from my theatre. I could never have made CITIZEN KANE with actors who were old hands at cinema because they would have said right off, 'Just what do you think we're doing?' My being a newcomer would have put them on guard and, at the same time, would have made a mess of the film."

And how did the cinematic innovations of his film come about? "I owe it to my ignorance," said Welles. "If this word seems inadequate to you, replace it with 'innocence.' I said to myself, 'This is what the camera should be really capable of doing, in a normal fashion.' When we were on the point of shooting the first sequence, I said, 'Let's do that!' Gregg Toland answered that it was impossible. I came back with, 'We can always try; we'll soon see; why not?' "

Welles was also asked if, during the shooting of the film, he had felt the sensation of creating a movie milestone. His reply was typically Welles—Welles being more of an enigma, really, than C. F. Kane could ever have hoped to be. "I never doubted it," said Welles, "for a single instant."

Before THE BIRTH OF A NATION: Paul Spehr
American Films, 1907-1914

THE BIRTH OF A NATION was hardly the birth of the American film. The movie industry was already gathering an imposing head of steam, and films were being produced with greater and greater frequency —and they were not all just giddy comedies. Part of the reason for overlooking the pre-BIRTH movies has been, of course, that few were around to be seen. That, at last, is changing.

Between 1907 and 1914 the American motion picture industry underwent a profound and astounding period of growth. In 1907 there were six American film "manufacturing companies," each producing about one film a week, supplemented by an equal number of importing firms who were bringing products from abroad. The manufacturers were at the culmination of a series of legal battles instituted by the Edison Company which effectively inhibited new producers from entering the competition. The films they produced were short, frequently less than 500 feet and almost never more than 1,000 feet. Travel and short newsreel items were mixed with modified vaudeville acts, melodramas, adventure or action stories, and comedies to make a varied fare available to the store-front theatres scattered across the country.

By 1914, *Moving Picture World* (July 11, 1914), a leading trade publication of the day, proclaimed the industry the fourth largest commercial interest in the United States and boasted that it "has shown a development that hitherto has not been equaled in the annals of business and that may well be termed the marvel of the Century. It was as if an Aladdin had rubbed a magic lamp, only there were many Aladdins and as many lamps. Some have amassed millions, and all the way down the scale are thousands of others who have gathered competences in varying amounts until we must pronounce the motion picture the most munificent of all Dame Fortune's vagaries, since through its channel she has most widely dispensed her bounty."

Thousands of new theatres were opening; film companies from the East were building huge studio complexes in Los Angeles; film executives and film stars were moving to new and palatial estates; and fan magazines were appearing on newsstands around the

The focal point of early American films: D. W. Griffith (right) and Billy Bitzer (left).

THE SQUAW MAN, 1914, Cecil B. De Mille's first film.

country. In the midst of this commercial revolution, D. W. Griffith was making THE BIRTH OF A NATION—a film which would combine commercial success with artistic achivement in a way no other film had done.

The achievement of this film has overshadowed the accomplishments, both commercial and artistic, of filmmakers who worked in the period immediately preceding its release. So strongly has it influenced everything that came afterward that there has been an inescapable temptation to use Griffith as the focal point for all of the cinematic achievements of the many thousands who worked in the movies before 1915.

Until recent years there have been very few pre-1915 films available for viewing. Most of the surviving films were viewed for their primitive humor and seldom regarded as part of the development of film art or industry. In this respect, the attitude toward this period is colored by the popular success of Charlie Chaplin and Mack Sennett. During the thirties and

forties and even well into the fifties, audiences associated all silent movies with comedies and tended to laugh at them all.

This appearance of frivolity is reinforced by the predominance of sentimental melodrama. However, if we look beyond the banal plot lines and the repetitive, heavy-handed humor of the time, it is possible to trace the beginnings of almost every technical development of the industry, including sound and color.

This is also the period when the role of the director became clearly established as an entity separate from the camera operators and business managers who frequently doubled in this capacity during the early years. In fact, specialization began in the industry at this time. (Stories are told of Broadway actors, lured to movies by the pay, who refused to build sets and paint scenery like the "picture players.")

But it is camera work and editing that make the most startling advances during this period. Most of these accomplishments have been attributed to Griffith, who publicly laid claim to the introduction of "large or close-up figures, distant views as represented first in RAMONA, the 'switchback,' sustained suspense, the 'fade out,' and restraint in expression, raising motion picture acting to the higher plane which has won for it recognition as a genuine art." (*Motion Picture World,* November 29, 1913.)

Griffith's place as the foremost director of his time and as the founder of the modern motion picture is by now well enough established so that film scholars can safely study the accomplishments of his contemporaries without fear of destroying the master. A viewing of a few films made by other companies in 1909 and 1910 occasionally shows a facility of camera work and editing frequently the equal of early Griffith films.

In the past the one major obstacle to the study of these early films has been the difficulty in locating them. Only a few of them were on safety film, and the nitrate was usually too difficult to handle. In the past few years, through the efforts of many people, an increasing number of these films are reappearing in archival collections and in 8mm and 16mm form in the commercial field. With a growing number of films available, scholars can now make more honest evalu-

The Thanhouser "Kidlet," who received much of her fame by being rescued from a real studio fire in 1913. Part of this fire was captured on film in the 1913 Thanhouser film in the collection, WHEN THE STUDIO BURNED.

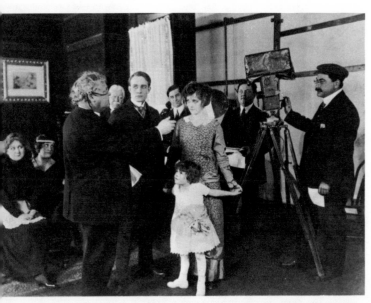

On the New Rochelle set of a Thanhouser film, about 1914. The "Kidlet," Helen Badgley, is in the center.

An early storefront studio. The Centaur Film Company in Bayonne, N.J., around 1907.

ations of the work done at film companies like Vitagraph, Selig, Essanay, Imp, Nestor, Crystal, Lubin, Edison, Kalem, Flying A, New York Motion Picture Company, and others, by directors like Kenean Buel, Sidney Olcott, Fred Balshofer, Francis Boggs, Rollin Sturgeon, Fred Thomson, Larry Trimble, Van Dyke Brooke, J. Stuart Blackton, G. M. Anderson, Marshall Neilan, Alice Guy-Blaché, and Thomas H. Ince.

Since the beginning of The American Film Institute's preservation program, more than 300 films from this early period have been added to the collection of film already at the Library of Congress. The value of this addition lies not in the number of films but in the companies represented. There are, for example, more than thirty early Universal productions and almost as many Vitagraphs. Previous to this time, the Library's collection included only half a dozen productions by each company. A significant number of films by Essanay, Pathé Frères, Gaumont, Kalem, Keystone, Lubin, Mutual, New York Motion Picture Company, Thanhouser, and others have also been acquired. These augment the almost 2,000 pre-1915 Biograph and Edison productions in the paper print and other early collections which were in the Library before the AFI's program began.

Most of the acquisitions from this period are original nitrate prints, and the first task is to make safety film copies so they can be available to scholars.

It is hoped that more of these pre-1915 productions will be located as their value becomes better known. Film historians already owe much to the efforts of the many film collectors whose interest in these antique curiosities preserved them through a period when they seemed of little interest to anyone.

Mary Pickford at Biograph: Legend and Legacy

Robert Cushman

Few actresses became genres, but Mary Pickford did. At first anonymous in the movies she made, she soon found that the audience had given her a name of its own: Mary. It stuck, and so did she, for one of the longest and most prolific careers in American cinema. It was a great moment for film preservation when Miss Pickford, who had personally preserved many of her films, allowed many more to be restored and placed in the Library of Congress. But her decision was, in fact, only the beginning of the story. . . .

From 1909 to 1912, Mary Pickford appeared in approximately 105 Biograph films, almost all of which were directed by D. W. Griffith. In many of these she had small parts or bit appearances, but in at least eighty of them, she played roles of major significance, and it is in these films that her great pantomimic talent was nurtured, developing into a whole new style of acting for the silent screen. These pictures represent the formative years of one of the most influential personalities in the history of motion pictures.

The Biograph studio was one of the most progressive film companies of the pioneer period. Its output represented the best film work coming out of America at the time. So it was a happy coincidence that Mary Pickford became devotedly associated with Biograph and Griffith, thereby giving her a wealth of fine films in which to develop her talents. By the time she was ready to make her first feature, she had learned the entire business of filmmaking from the master himself, D. W. Griffith. Her knowledge grew with his; she learned infinitely from him and was inspired to remain in film for life.

In a space of three years, Mary Pickford played an extraordinary variety of roles. She appeared in comedies, romances, action adventures, dramas, and period pieces. Contrary to popular belief, Griffith did not cast her only as an ingenue or young lady, but allowed her to play almost every kind of woman: she played "Faro Kate," a shiftless claim jumper in WITH THE ENEMY'S HELP; the Mexican heroine of RAMONA; and an Indian maiden in SONG OF THE WILDWOOD FLUTE, A PUEBLO LEGEND, and

Mary Pickford in THE MENDER OF NETS, 1912.

W. Chrystie Miller and Mary Pickford in THE UNWELCOME GUEST, *made in October of 1912, but not released until March of 1913.*

many other pictures. In WILFUL PEGGY, she was a spirited, temperamental Irish lass; a sultry vamp in THE SORROWS OF THE UNFAITHFUL; a doleful wallflower in A PLAIN SONG; and a cynical, jaded shrew in THE FEMALE OF THE SPECIES.

In 1922, Miss Pickford purchased the negatives of about eighty of her most important Biographs, lest others capitalize on their re-release, and she has kept them under perfect storage conditions to this day. By 1969, she had managed to have preservation copies made of about thirty of these films, and at that point The American Film Institute persuaded Miss Pickford to allow them to do the preservation work on the remaining fifty titles. The entire collection has, therefore, been converted to safety film and is preserved for all time.

The process of beginning with Miss Pickford's original negatives and ending with projectable safety prints was painstaking and complex. First, all 50,000 feet of the delicate and highly flammable sixty-year-old nitrate negatives were shipped from Los Angeles to the AFI in Washington. These negatives, made before four sprocket holes per frame became standard for 35mm film, had only one hole per frame; hence the problem of printing from one-perforation nitrate negative to four-perforation safety stock. This dilemma was solved by Donald Malkames, who owns the original Biograph printer and adapted it to do the job. All the negatives were then sent to his workshop in New York, where he produced fine-grain master prints of exceptional quality.

On first consideration, one might think that the restoration was completed at this point. But preservation (the conversion of nitrate film to safety film) and restoration (the construction of a final projectable print) are two entirely separate matters, as I learned when I offered to carry out the work, and in the case of these Biographs, the fun was just about to begin. I quickly discovered that almost all of the negatives had been spliced into tinting sequence rather than continuity (chronological) sequence; therefore, of course, the new safety prints were also out of sequence. Next, I realized that the titles for the films presented several other problems: some of the films had complete title footage; others simply had one-frame title indicators

Henry B. Walthall, Mary Pickford, and Walter Miller in THE INFORMER, 1912.

Mary Pickford in FRIENDS, 1912.

Mary Pickford and Kate Bruce in RAMONA, 1910.

spliced into the negative; other films which had had titles when released now had no titles surviving at all; still others had misleading and badly written titles spliced into them to pad the films for reissue as two-reelers in the teens by another company, the original Biograph titles having been discarded.

The job of putting the new prints into proper sequence and locating the original title material became a major undertaking. The problem was solved when we learned that the Biograph Company had submitted complete prints of most of their films on paper rolls to the Library of Congress for copyrighting when the films were originally released. These paper prints survive and have since been printed onto 16mm film, are projectable, and were therefore usable as reference prints for the sequencing of the films. These 16mm prints, however, often contained incomplete title material; so it was necessary to consult the original paper rolls for the reconstruction of the proper titles and the location of their positions in the original release prints. Thanks to the happy coincidence of the existence of these reference paper prints, I completed the final step of sequencing and titling, a job that turned into a ten-week project, and now the preservation of all fifty films is complete.

For future film scholars, the value of Miss Pickford's donation of these Biograph negatives is inestimable. Not since the release of the films has it been possible to see such fine quality prints of so much of the early work of Griffith and Pickford. At last, Billy Bitzer's dazzling photography of the Biograph years may be appreciated as it was meant to be, for these prints are probably the best surviving material from so early a period. Audiences of today may have the unique opportunity to see what these rare examples of the birth of cinema art actually looked like when released. The finest details are visible, and much of the footage looks as though it could have been shot yesterday.

Alfred Paget and Mary Pickford in IOLA'S PROMISE, 1912.

Mary Pickford in A PUEBLO LEGEND, 1912.

Mary Pickford (left) and Grace Henderson
(right) in JUST LIKE A WOMAN, 1912.

Kevin Brownlow

THE WISHING RING

World Film Corporation. 1914.
Director: Maurice Tourneur.
Based on a story by Owen Davis.
Cast: Alec B. Francis, Vivian Martin, Chester Barnett, Johnny Hines.

A   B   C

G   H   I

Films in the AFI Collection have been found in attics, garages, and caves—in places as varied as New Jersey, Australia, and Czechoslovakia. Sometimes films are rescued at the last minute from death by fire or nitrate disintegration. Kevin Brownlow came across a copy of Maurice Tourneur's THE WISHING RING by accident, and almost ignored the find, until he found out what it was.

My fascination with Maurice Tourneur was fired more by his potential than by his actual work. William K. Everson's program notes for LORNA DOONE caught my imagination: "Pictorial beauty has always been the strongest point of any Tourneur film. The shots of the sinister Doones, sitting on horseback on the crest of misty hills; the wrecked coach in the sea; the dramatic silhouettes against stark rock cliffs; the lovely pastorale scenes and the magnificently composed interiors all compare more than favorably with the *best* that Murnau, von Gerlach, von Sternberg and all the other great (but more celebrated) visual directors have ever given us. . . ."

LORNA DOONE, when I finally saw it, had many

D

E

F

K

A short episode from the first reel of *THE WISHING RING* which is indicative of Tourneur's skill:

A. *Medium close shot. Giles is pulled out of a tavern by the militia. A woman runs out to give him his hat. On her movement back, we cut to . . .*

B. *Close shot. A woman, incensed by the noise Giles and his friends have been making, appears at the window with a jug of water.*

C. *Close shot. A man at another window sniggers in anticipation.*

D. *Medium close shot. Giles, struggling furiously with his captors, is dragged along the street.*

E. *Close shot. The woman empties the jug.*

F. & G. *Medium close shot. The water splashes over Giles and the militiamen. They gesticulate angrily upwards.*

H. *The empty window.*

I. *The man at the other window slams it shut and peers through the glass.*

J. *Medium close shot. Giles is frog-marched off. On the action of the group moving round a building, cut to . . .*

K. *Giles is thrown into a cell.*

moments of great beauty, but it lacked the magic that I hoped for. Comforting myself with the fact that every great director makes an occasional poor picture, I waited for the moment when I would see a Tourneur masterpiece.

When it came, I almost ignored it. I discovered a defunct 16mm film library in the North of England. Rare films, tinted and in excellent condition, were being sold for £1 a reel. One mysterious title was THE WISHING RING. Examining the main title against the light, I read AN IDYLL OF OLD ENGLAND. Assuming it to be one of those soporific British silents, I replaced it on the shelf and left for London.

Vivian Martin.

£5 in cash. The film arrived in pristine condition on amber-toned base, and proved to be the only copy in existence.

THE WISHING RING turned out to be an enchanting, will-o'-the-wisp comedy-drama; the lightness of touch, however, concealed a sophisticated knowledge of filmmaking. Modern audiences may notice nothing unusual about the film. They enjoy its freshness and impish vitality, but since there are no striking innovations or dramatic effects, they don't regard it as an important picture. Yet pictorially, and from the editing point of view, THE WISHING RING is sprinkled with surprises.

Tourneur's method of cutting swiftly between various elements within a scene became common with certain directors later in the silent period. The technique of time-cutting, linking two shots separated by time without using a time-lapse device such as a fade or dissolve, did not become common, or even acceptable, until the early sixties. THE WISHING RING contains only a few such technical flourishes, but it is a most accomplished production for 1914. Pictorially exquisite (cameraman John van den Broek was an essential ally for Tourneur's pictorial eye), it proves that Tourneur was one of the men who introduced visual beauty to the American screen. American pictures of 1914 were often well photographed, but I have seen few to compare for sheer visual elegance with Tourneur's.

The players—Chester Barnett, Alec B. Francis, and Vivian Martin—are directed to give completely naturalistic performances; nearly sixty years after its release, the acting seems witty and spontaneous. Vivian Martin was one of the actresses who, given Mary Pickford roles (every company had at least one Pickford substitute), could imbue them with her own personality. Judging from this film, she could have had a scintillating career. Unfortunately she left the picture business in the early twenties and returned to the stage.

THE WISHING RING was blown up to 35mm and preserved in The American Film Institute Collection. It is a tribute to the film's photographic excellence that it could stand the strain and still look as enchanting as ever.

At the British Film Institute, a historian, Denis Gifford, was building up a gigantic index to all British feature films. I mentioned this one. "It's pretty old," I told him, "probably pre-1920." He jotted down the title and reported back that it was not a British film. It appeared to be an American five-reel production of 1914, directed by Maurice Tourneur.

Horrified that my oversight might have lost me this rarity, I wrote a hasty letter to the library, enclosing

The Hal Roach Shorts
Leonard Maltin

As the Hal Roach studio turned out comedy shorts, it also turned out new talent. Feature film directors like Leo McCarey and George Marshall began their careers working on the Roach two-reelers. But the Roach studio was more than just a training ground. The comedy shorts were ends in themselves, making the most of talents like Laurel and Hardy and Charley Chase. Laurel and Hardy would also go on to feature films in the thirties, but they never really sustained the success they had reached in the Hal Roach shorts.

To call the Hal Roach studio a "comedy factory" is to give the impression that films were turned out on an assembly line. Nothing could be further from the truth. The Roach studio specialized in comedy short subjects, but Hal Roach realized that putting pressure on his employees would create a poor atmosphere for making comedies. Instead, the feeling on the Roach lot was one of fun, and this mood in turn was conveyed to the audience when they watched the studio's product.

It may sound like a cliche to say that the studio was "one big happy family," but it was true. There were few hard-and-fast rules. Comics Charley Chase, Stan Laurel, Edgar Kennedy, and Billy Gilbert all worked as directors and gagmen, while writer-directors Charles Rogers, George Marshall, and Gordon Douglas all turned up on camera from time to time. The extras in Roach films were usually the friends and family of the comedy stars!

Hal Roach was something of an enigma; the founder of the studio, he would occasionally get the urge to direct, but boredom would set in about noontime, and he would turn to whoever was handy to finish the film. Many a directing career was launched in this manner, and among the directors who emerged from the Roach lot were George Stevens (who started there as a cameraman) Leo McCarey, George Marshall, and Gordon Douglas.

While one would generally categorize the Roach films as "slapstick comedies," they were quite different from the films of Mack Sennett, the father of screen comedy. Roach's films had more polish than Sennett's, relying much more on characterization than

Stan Laurel and Oliver Hardy in THE FINISHING TOUCH, 1928.

just a string of gags.

Charley Chase was the first exponent of this kind of comedy at the Roach studio; unlike most comedians of the day, he wore no funny make-up or costume. Indeed, he was quite handsome, and the laughs in his films are derived from outlandish situations in which he happened to find himself. Chase hit his stride in the twenties working with young Leo McCarey (who later said, "Chase taught me all I know") on such classic comedies as MIGHTY LIKE A MOOSE, BAD BOY, DOG SHY, and HIS WOODEN WEDDING.

Laurel and Hardy leaned more toward slapstick, but they, too, with such directors as Fred Guiol, Clyde Bruckman, and James Parrott, realized that **147**

APPLES TO YOU, 1934.

"*Our Gang.*"

148

Thelma Todd, Billy Gilbert, James Burtis, and ZaSu Pitts in BARGAIN OF A CENTURY, 1933.

speed was not the essence of comedy, as some film-makers seemed to think. When they staged a pie-throwing melee in THE BATTLE OF THE CENTURY, it was funny because of its structure, starting out with Ollie's banana peel tripping a man carrying a trayful of pies. In retaliation, he slowly walks toward Ollie and hits him with a pie, while Ollie does nothing to stop him. Then Ollie saunters over, picks up a pie, and throws it—missing his adversary and drawing an innocent passerby into the fracas. And so it builds, until an entire city block is caught in the crossfire. This systematic destruction was the basis of their best films: TWO TARS, BIG BUSINESS, A PERFECT DAY.

When the talkie revolution hit Hollywood, the Roach craftsmen were among the few to realize, right from the start, that they didn't have to change their com-edies to suit talking pictures. They already had hilari-ous card-titles (written by studio wit H. M. Walker); this would become their dialogue. As for the rest—well, the sound would just come naturally. The Roach people learned to use sound and not let it use them.

Laurel and Hardy flourished in the sound era, re-fining their style with the help of voices that perfectly matched their characters. Charley Chase continued to make his bright two-reel comedies, occasionally burst-ing into song. "Our Gang" carried on, discovering such remarkable young performers as Jackie Cooper, Dickie Moore, and George "Spanky" McFarland. New stars came to the Roach lot—vivacious Thelma Todd, teamed first with ZaSu Pitts and then with Patsy Kelly; Billy Gilbert, Ben Blue, Irvin S. Cobb, and others.

There were always new surprises: Laurel and Hardy making a gag appearance as hitchhikers in Charley Chase's ON THE WRONG TREK; Chase directing Thelma Todd, ZaSu Pitts, and Billy Gilbert in the hilarious BARGAIN OF THE CENTURY; Billy Gil-bert playing the burlesque king, Pinsky, who adds chorus girls and a runway to a production of "The Barber of Seville" in APPLES TO YOU; "Our Gang" alumnae Mickey Daniels and Mary Kornman looking back at themselves as kids in the "Boy Friends" short, TOO MANY WOMEN.

The infectious background music by Marvin Hatley, the marvelous stock company of supporting players (Charlie Hall, Mae Busch, Tiny Sandford, Harry Bowen, Harry Bernard), the skill of the writers and directors, and effortless charm of the leading comics all combined to make the Hal Roach comedies the best in Hollywood.

Eventually, Roach phased out short-subject produc-tion to move on to feature films like TOPPER, ONE MILLION B.C., and OF MICE AND MEN (also in the AFI Collection). He met with considerable suc-cess, but it could never be the same. His studio had made the two-reel comedy a fine art, and they would never duplicate that success in any other field.

BROADWAY

Tom Shales

Universal Pictures. 1929.
Director: Paul Fejos.
Screenplay: Edward T. Lowe, Jr., and Charles Furthman.
Cast: Glenn Tryon, Evelyn Brent, Merna Kennedy, Thomas Jackson, Robert Ellis.

"I love you little fella. . . . I'd do murder for you."
Love in the twenties. BROADWAY, in which that
dialogue is uttered by a tacky gangster, conveys the
tawdry innocence of that decade with songs, dances,
and shootings. As a film, it's an interesting crossroads
item, but it may be more significant as a summation
of period passions—as Americans looked with titillated
alarm at the big city growing ever bigger in an in-
creasingly urban society. Broadway was the wicked,
glamorous, wish-fulfillment boulevard that brought it
all together, and it replaced Main Street, U.S.A., as
our most representative stretch of asphalt.

Robert Ellis (left) and Merna Kennedy in BROADWAY.

In 1929, some people were still waiting for the talkies to die out, like all silly fads do, so that the silents could return to dominance. No one then was precisely and positively sure where the movies were going next. BROADWAY, directed by Paul Fejos in 1929, reflects this ambivalence and the fact that many theatre owners had not yet been able to install expensive sound equipment. It was released in both silent and sound versions; it had a last reel in two-color Technicolor; it was both a musical and, somehow, not a musical. It was truly a just-in-case picture, alternately stagy and cinematic, and in many ways a summation of several genres.

BROADWAY can't technically be called a musical because its songs could be removed without changing the substance of the film at all. All of them are staged as just that—staged songs, being viewed by an audience in a graphically twenties nightclub. The film has some of the characteristics of a musical in its subject matter—backstage politics, melodrama, and intrigue—but it takes the saga of broken and bleeding hearts more seriously than most musicals. Still, its essential philosophy is not unlike that expressed in the typical Busby Berkeley film several years later—when Dick Powell sings of 42nd Street "The big parade goes on for years! It's a rhapsody of laughter and tears. . . ." The established truth of the day was that Broadway was a wicked, worldly place where life was acted out with as much fervor and drama backstage as onstage. And that, further, it symbolized and epitomized real life; it was real life with the edges sharpened, the

pulse quickened, the crises more critical, the vagaries of fate—and fame—even more relentless.

The theme is established from the pre-credits shot of a midnight reveller, who looks like the devil, stalking through a convincing miniature of Times Square (which would turn up later and briefly in KING OF JAZZ). As the city lights up, the specter sprinkles it with, apparently, champagne, or some other vital juice, and he laughs maniacally as he does it—Ah, the hearts that will break! The heads that will roll! The hopes that will shatter! This is the same Broadway that Charles King has summarized and defined in the title song of the musical BROADWAY MELODY.

151

Glenn Tryon and Merna Kennedy in BROADWAY.

Almost every musical before 1930 was fashioned as a more or less mawkish tribute to the boulevard of broken dreams that slices mean old Manhattan down the approximate middle. The cinema, at least the new sound cinema, was still widely viewed as the next best thing—a viable alternative—to the theatrical experience, inferior to it and no more than a replica of it.

BROADWAY has little visual dynamism. It is encumbered with long, static two-shots that seem transplanted intact from the original play by Philip Dunning, George Abbott, and Jed Harris. Yet, there are moments. One of the musical numbers is preceded by a dramatic camera zoom into and through the curtain—we travel from the fantasy world of the stage to the real world of backstage, where song and dance man Roy Lane (Glenn Tryon) is changing clothes for another number. He shifts his expression from grim concern to synthetic smile—for the crowd—as the camera zooms back out again, to await his entrance. Later, there will be a dizzying pan—it seems like a full 360-degree revolution—of the mammoth and orgiastic Paradise Club, where the story is set.

Predictably, the film is preoccupied with show-must-go-on schtick. While gangsters are matter-of-factly murdering each other in the backstage offices, the ridiculous revue continues. Hero Lane is a trouper to the marrow of his bones, and he says so in an emotional speech just after a crisis and prior to yet another entrance. "And even if a Jane I'd pinned all my hopes on was goin' to hell," he says, in pre-Production-Code candor, "I'd still go on and do my best!" To his fellow performers, the chorus cuties, he commands with cornball bravado: "Cut 'em deep and let 'em bleed"—referring, of course, to the audience.

Still, Lane is not mere stereotype. The screenplay catches him offguard, and Tryon's rather desperate performance gives him his own reality. We see in him a sense of failure not unlike that of the alcoholic Norman Maine in both versions of A STAR IS BORN, except that Lane is not an alcoholic. He is, though, a brash ham. When envisioning the big time for himself and his pretty partner Billie Moore (Merna Kennedy), he shouts, "I can see our names in lights right now—Roy Lane—and company!"

Glenn Tryon and Merna Kennedy in BROADWAY.

The dialogue written for the film by Edward T. Lowe, Jr., is a virtual glossary of period slang, and it makes even the flattest scenes worth listening to. The words and phrases fly fast and furiously: "weisenheimer," "rough stuff," "a big rounder," "swell fella," "sez you," "runnin' wild," "gum it," "I'm strong for ya," "floorflusher," "hitched up," "shoot square," "tie on the feedbag," "razzin'," "nix," "on the fritz," and those famous last words, "I'll bet my winter underwear . . ." The cliches get a bit thick, too, replete with a reference to "your poor old grey-haired mother" and Billie's not so original declaration that "I'm not that kind of a girl." Even when it's self-consciously snappy, though, the dialogue has a colorful ring. Gangster Steve, hooked on Billie himself, says it this way: "I love you little fella, I love you. I'd do murder for you."

There are details in the lives of the little people that help relieve the monotony of the central story and give BROADWAY something of the panoramic scope it aspires to. The print secured by The American Film Institute is a crisp black-and-white beauty that unfortunately lacks the closing reel—the color production number. The hunt goes on.

Joseph E. Dispenza

Making It Wholesome: The Owens Collection

A paint brush offers such an easy way to reform the world. From THE HOMEKEEPING OF JIM, *1920.*

Just as it has always been a widespread suspicion that Hollywood was determined to undermine American morality, so have there been many attempts to use film for social uplift, for encouragement of prosocial behavior, for the betterment, ostensibly, of the brain. Today cable television is viewed by many as the medium of a new millenium—the technological miracle that will bind us together in righteous harmony. Not so long ago, that's what some people expected from the motion picture, and existing examples of films made with this purpose offer subtle insights into the American mind.

In the early twenties, while regular moviegoers were viewing the bathroom-and-bedroom melodramas of Cecil B. De Mille and the raucous urban antics of Mack Sennett's Kops, school children and church groups were being exposed to a different kind of film entertainment. Non-theatrical distribution of "educational" films was originally meant as a church-supervised alternative to the sometimes morally questionable features in theatrical release.

The dream of John E. Edgerton, a Southern industrialist, pillar of the Methodist Church, and president of the powerful National Association of Manufacturers, was for the Church to enter the motion picture business on a competitive basis with the theatres. (It is interesting to observe that the late J. Arthur Rank, noted British producer, began his motion picture empire with the same uplifting objectives.) Edgerton was once quoted as saying that he had at his disposal 10,000 YMCA buildings and church auditoriums, and that he would "turn these into motion picture theatres and then proceed to produce suitable films." The American Motion Picture Corporation, begun in 1923, brought together Edgerton's dream with Paul Smith's Church Film Company. Many of the short films distributed through the non-theatrical routes created by the American Motion Picture Corporation are in the Owens Collection, which consists of films distributed by Henry Owens, Sr., of Providence, Rhode Island, in the twenties and saved by his son, Henry Jr., on the original early "safety" film stock.

Lon Chaney in THE LIGHT OF FAITH, *1922.*

The Owens Collection, acquired by The American Film Institute with the cooperation of The Rhode Island Historical Society, is a fascinating library of these early films. Some indication of its content can be seen from a few of the titles; AGRICULTURAL RESOURCES; AMERICAN GARDENS WITH PROTECTIVE SOIL; FROM TREE TO SUGAR; CATERPILLARS, BUTTERFLIES AND FLOWERS; and LAND OF MANY WATERS are examples of short instructional films dealing with conservation, biology, and earth science. An interesting subgenre of nature films includes titles such as LAND OF OPPORTUNITY, MOTHERHOOD IN NATURE, and PROVIDENCE OF NATURE, instructional entries with religious and nationalistic overtones.

More specific religious films constitute perhaps the backbone of the collection: THE GOOD SAMARITAN, IMMORTALITY, IN THE MASTER'S FOOTSTEPS, THE LORD IS MY SHEPHERD, OPEN THINE EYES, and ST. THOMAS. The films are generally ten minutes in length and often offer a simple illustration of a psalm or a pious story from Scripture. All of the religious films seem to reflect a Protestant viewpoint. THE WIDOW'S MITE and SPIRITUAL LAW IN A MATERIAL WORLD, for example, take strong Protestant stands in describing the moral obligations of the country.

Films about sports are common, and titles such as AMERICAN BOY OUTDOORS, BASEBALL IN SLOW MOTION (demonstrated by Babe Ruth), and FRENCH GIRLS GO IN FOR SPORT (which has the pace and tone of newsreels produced in the twenties) illustrate the place of sports and related activities in the development of good, clean-cut American youth. FRENCH GIRLS GO IN FOR SPORT is one of a number of films that take a culturally superior attitude. At one point, the title tells us that although French girls are not quite as robust and healthy as British girls, the young ladies from France make valiant attempts at field sports. A similar condescending attitude permeates NORTH AMERICA, CENTER OF THE WORLD NEIGHBORHOOD; FAMILIAR FOODS FROM FOREIGN LANDS; and QUAINT PEOPLE. At times the cultural bias encourages common stereotypes, as in SACRED ANIMALS AND NA-

E. K. Lincoln and Hope Hampton in THE LIGHT OF FAITH, 1922.

TIVE SPORTS OF INDIA and SHANGHAI, a travelogue that also includes some information on Singapore.

The Owens Collection also contains a fair sampling of purely entertainment films. For instance, the inclusion of PECK'S BAD BOY (1921), with Jackie Coogan in the title role, might have been justified by the fact that it was a literary classic of sorts based on the long-lived play of the same title which must have had runs in every opera and vaudeville house of the country during the late 19th and early 20th Centuries. The same could be said of a four-reel ALICE IN WONDERLAND. But three Chaplin films made at Mutual and a number of cartoons (including a vintage 1922 Disney) seem to have been placed in the traveling program to liven up the rather heavy doses of religious and patriotic instruction.

Jackie Coogan and Wheeler Oakman in PECK'S BAD BOY, 1921.

Two short dramatic pieces are of special interest. Both THE HOMEKEEPING OF JIM (1920) and THE LIGHT OF FAITH (a recut and newly titled version of Clarence Brown's 1922 THE LIGHT IN THE DARK) are filmic parables that take up the themes of personal sacrifice, cooperation, and the role of religion in life. In the first picture Jim is married to a nagging wife who is angry most of the time because Jim will not repair the family sofa. He is tempted to leave his unhappy home to wander freely on the open road, but puts it off until he has fixed the sofa. When his wife discovers the repaired sofa, she cheerily sews a cover for it. Their daughter decides to make a pillow for the sofa instead of running off with the town ruffian.

The repair of the sofa sets off a chain reaction that includes, finally, the repair and painting of the entire house, inside and out. In the end Jim is a happy man, fulfilling all of his responsibilities as husband and father—and all because of a sofa. THE HOMEKEEPING OF JIM is particularly interesting because it is one of a handful of films produced for *The Youth's Companion*, that stalwart educator, entertainer, and propagandizer of the American ideal in youth, which had a publishing career of more than a century before folding in 1928. THE HOMEKEEPING OF JIM epitomizes this magazine's Victorian editorial policy.

THE LIGHT OF FAITH is a beautifully tinted short feature starring Lon Chaney as a boarder who falls in love with a new girl in town. The girl, played by Hope Hampton, is in failing health, feeling herself abandoned by her fiance, a wealthy gentleman who has discovered the legendary Holy Grail. The Grail is known to have magical powers. Chaney steals the cup and brings it to the girl, who is miraculously healed. The fiance files charges against Chaney, but at the trial the "evidence"—the Holy Grail itself—is taken back up to heaven on a beatific beam of light, instigating a change of heart, and all are forgiven.

Both films are fairly representative of the Owens Collection and of the many short films in non-theatrical distribution during the twenties. THE HOMEKEEPING OF JIM is a dramatic sermon on the duties of the head-of-household: a remarkably economical portrayal of the modes of familial conduct held up for emulation in the third decade of this century in America. THE LIGHT OF FAITH is more specifically religious, dealing primarily with the place of faith in day-to-day living. The healing of the sick by the chalice used at the Last Supper; the purity of love relationships; and the final exemplary mercy of the court in the case of Lon Chaney's theft, demonstrate clearly the effects of faith and the rewards of piety.

These "educational" short films seem quaint today, but they stand as interesting documentation of American cultural history, recalling an age when life was slower, more settled, and a great deal more innocent.

Jackie Coogan in PECK'S BAD BOY.

An advertising lobby card.

Joel E. Siegel

Val Lewton

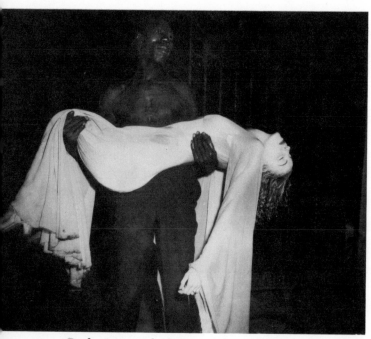

Darby Jones and Christine Gordon in I WALKED WITH A ZOMBIE, 1943

While we continue to award accolades to illustrious directors, it is important to remember that there were creative producers as well. Thomas H. Ince was one. In the forties, Val Lewton was another, a man whose distinctive identity shaped the films he produced, and whose artistic guidance launched subsequently celebrated directors like Robert Wise on their own careers.

One can hardly claim to "rediscover" Val Lewton, the writer-producer whose inventive series of low-budget RKO films in the forties won the praise of both popular audiences and intellectuals. And yet, for all of the legend surrounding Lewton's career—kept alive in the writings of James Agee and Manny Farber, and by the Lewtonesque protagonist of Vincente Minnelli's THE BAD AND THE BEAUTIFUL—some of Lewton's very best work is virtually unknown today. The American Film Institute has preserved the negatives of Lewton's eleven RKO productions so that one day scholars and audiences will have the opportunity to study Lewton's achievement.

Lewton was born in Yalta, Russia in 1904. His mother brought him to New York City in 1906, where she was reunited with her sister, the celebrated actress, Alla Nazimova. In the twenties, after a year at Columbia University Journalism School, Lewton left school to embark upon a series of literary activities. By the age of thirty, he had published nine novels—in genres ranging from historical romance to social realism to pornography—as well as a collection of poems, six nonfiction volumes on topics ranging from Casanova's women to the history of cosmetics, and over one hundred articles in magazines like *American Mercury, Cosmopolitan,* and *The Little Review.* During this period, he spent six years working for the MGM Publicity Department in New York where he turned out weekly serializations of MGM films as well as radio dramatizations. In 1933, he wrote the three weekly episodes of a soap opera, "The Luck of Joan Christopher."

Lewton first came to Hollywood in 1934 to write a screen adaptation of Gogol's *Taras Bulba* for producer David Selznick. Although the screenplay was never filmed, Selznick was so impressed with Lewton's

158

Christine Gordon and Frances Dee in I WALKED WITH A ZOMBIE.

Skelton Knaggs and Richard Dix in THE GHOST SHIP, 1943.

Boris Karloff and Russell Wade in THE BODY SNATCHER, 1945.

talent and intelligence that he kept him on as head of the Selznick-International Story Department. During his eight years with Selznick, Lewton made a number of significant contributions to Selznick's productions. He produced the second unit of A TALE OF TWO CITIES, working with director Jacques Tourneur and, uncredited, wrote several scenes for GONE WITH THE WIND.

In 1942, Lewton was asked by Charles Koerner to head a ''B''-movie production unit at RKO which would turn out thrillers to compete with Universal for the horror market. Lewton would have to work under severe limitations—very low budgets, running times under seventy minutes—and the titles of his productions were to be dictated in advance by the studio. Despite these limitations and partly because of them, Lewton managed to create a series of sensitive, unexpectedly poetic psychological thrillers.

The producer realized immediately that, if work of any quality were to be done, he would have to surround himself with a company of talented, sympathetic people. He began with director Jacques Tourneur, writer DeWitt Bodeen, and editor Mark Robson, fresh from the recently dismissed Orson Welles Mercury Theatre group at RKO. The first production was CAT PEOPLE (1942) with Simone Simon, an eerie, atmospheric chiller about a woman haunted by the fear that, if aroused, she had the power to transform herself into a deadly cat. The film, which cost $134,000, grossed several million dollars. Lewton and Tourneur continued their collaboration with I WALKED WITH A ZOMBIE (1943), an adaptation of *Jane Eyre* set in the tropics and visually one of the most intoxicating American sound films, as well as with the moody, terrifying THE LEOPARD MAN (1943).

Tourneur left the Lewton unit to direct bigger productions at RKO, and several new directors emerged— Mark Robson and Robert Wise, also a Mercury Theatre alumnus. Lewton continued to make thrillers after Tourneur's departure including the seldom-revived, extremely intricate THE SEVENTH VICTIM (1943), about devil worship in Manhattan (and with ZOMBIE, Lewton's masterpiece), ISLE OF THE DEAD (1945), and THE BODY SNATCHER (1945), based upon the Robert Louis Stevenson story. In addition, he began expanding his range by attacking other kinds of material. With Robert Wise and Gunther Fritsch, Lewton produced the deceptively titled CURSE OF THE CAT PEOPLE (1944), a delicately wrought and partly autobiographical investigation of the problems of an imaginative child. YOUTH RUNS WILD (1944, directed by Robson) is an unsuccessful but impressive study of wartime juvenile delinquency which prefigures films of the Italian Neorealists. MADEMOISELLE FIFI (1944, directed by Wise), adapted from two Maupassant stories, is an eloquent indictment of the behavior of the French bourgeoisie during the Franco-Prussian War and, incidentally, the least expensive costume picture since the days of silent films.

Particularly interesting among the Lewton productions of this period is THE GHOST SHIP (1943) a Conradian psychological story about a murderously obsessed sea captain which was withdrawn from distribution following a lawsuit in 1945 and which has not been exhibited theatrically since that time.

Following his last RKO production, BEDLAM (1946), an uneven but memorable story about the infamous English madhouse, St. Mary of Bethlehem, Lewton went on to make films at Paramount, MGM, and Universal, which, for a variety of reasons, were mostly unsuccessful. He was preparing THE FOUR POSTER and MY SIX CONVICTS for producer Stanley Kramer at the time of his death in 1951.

Lewton was one of Hollywood's rare *creative* producers. Directors Tourneur, Wise, and Robson subsequently made films of considerable individuality but, in their work for Lewton, the producer's imaginative vision is predominant. Lewton's sensibility is present in every frame of his films—in the suggestive use of shadow and sound, in the scrupulous attention to detail, and in the literate screenplays. (He contributed extensively to the screenplays of all of his films, either anonymously or under the pseudonym "Carlos Keith.") In less than four years at RKO, Lewton created an

Boris Karloff and Helene Thimig in ISLE OF THE DEAD, 1945.

impressive and important body of work, a collection of films which James Agee praised for being "so consistently alive, limber, poetic, humane, so eager toward the possiblities of the screen and so resolutely against the grain of all we have learned to expect from the big studios."

Today's moviegoers can seldom see more than a suggestion of the meticulousness of Lewton's films. A few of the Lewton titles exist in 35mm, and the others are available only in shoddily executed 16mm television reductions. Hopefully, in time, The American Film Institute will restore the complete RKO Lewton series, including such rarities as THE SEVENTH VICTIM, MADEMOISELLE FIFI, and the virtually "lost" THE GHOST SHIP.

Vivian Reed, the Oz Girl.

The original opening title of HIS MAJESTY,
THE SCARECROW OF OZ.

"I thought Oz was a great Head," said Dorothy.

"I thought Oz was a lovely Lady," said the Scarecrow.

"And I thought Oz was a terrible Beast," said the Tin Woodman.

"And I thought Oz was a Ball of Fire," exclaimed the Lion.

"No; you are all wrong," said the little man meekly. "I have been making believe."

Making believe was what L. Frank Baum did best. He did it with some reluctance. He had no intention of publishing sequels to his book The Wizard of Oz, *but the children of the nation literally demanded them. It was only natural that Baum would turn to film as another way of liberating his fantasy. Film was the magic of the moment. Though the Oz films never approached the success of the Oz books, they explored some of the cinematic possibilities of visual illusion, and their survival recreates a time when the movies were only beginning to demonstrate their aptness for making believe.*

Among the more curious acquisitions of The American Film Institute Collection are two feature films made by L. Frank Baum's Oz Film Manufacturing Company in 1914 and 1915: HIS MAJESTY, THE SCARE-CROW OF OZ (also known as THE NEW WIZARD OF OZ), and THE MAGIC CLOAK OF OZ.

In the spring of 1914, Baum, deciding to capitalize on the success of his Oz novels and the stage plays he had produced from them all over the country, formed his own company, Oz Films, with the financial support of the "Uplifters," a fraternal club to which he belonged. Purchasing part of an old estate in Los Angeles, the corporation set up a rather posh studio, complete with the largest enclosed stage in the country, concrete tanks that could be filled with water to create "rivers," and "shower-baths and hot and cold running water" in all of the dressing rooms. Joseph F. Macdonald was hired to direct, and Oz Films began to produce spinoff features from Baum's novels.

The result of Baum's labors are charming films, originally and optimistically aimed at the family trade.

Fred Woodward in his various roles in HIS MAJESTY,
THE SCARECROW OF OZ with Mae Wells (left)
and Vivian Reed (below).

Frank Moore as His Majesty, The Scarecrow of Oz.

However, since the features were somewhat short in production values and had the overall look of one- and two-reelers produced about five years earlier in the industry, they proved difficult to distribute. THE PATCHWORK GIRL ·OF OZ, the company's first completed feature, was released by Paramount under duress. Paramount found the family and children's market just about as thankless as it is today (well-meaning family-oriented production firms still find themselves on shaky financial grounds in the current adult film market) and refused to market Baum's second feature, THE MAGIC CLOAK OF OZ. Frustrated, Baum cut MAGIC CLOAK into two shorter versions and sold the exclusive distribution rights on a "states rights" (independent distribution, region by region) basis. The AFI Collection's print is one of these cut versions, released in the early twenties by the American Motion Picture Company, a distribution firm which catered to schools and churches.

Ignoring all these distribution problems, the company went ahead and produced a third five-reel feature, HIS MAJESTY, THE SCARECROW OF OZ. The story was a combination of elements from Baum's original novel, *The Wizard of Oz*, and several of its successors. The film was technically and dramatically more successful than its predecessors; and, after opening an office in New York to be closer to the distributors, the Oz Film Company managed to convince Alliance to distribute the picture.

By this time the corporate owners of Oz Films awoke to the problems of trying to sell basically children's films to an audience that wanted adult subjects. THE LAST EGYPTIAN, a costume melodrama based on an anonymous novel of Baum's, was produced and released with moderate success. A series of four one-reel fairy tales followed this.

The studio was closed for several months while negotiations with New York distributors were again undertaken. Sensing a victory, it reopened in April of 1915 to film another dramatic feature, THE GREY NUN OF BELGIUM. With a timely World War I plot and even more improved production techniques, the film should have proved successful, but it was never released due to the reluctance of the distributors to swallow more of the Oz Film Company's near disas-

Mildred Harris (Button Bright), Violet Macmillan (Dorothy), and Frank Moore.

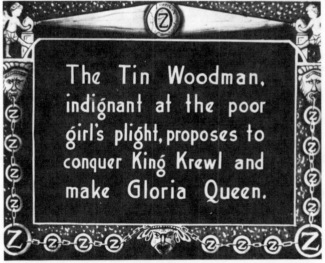

An original title from HIS MAJESTY, THE SCARECROW OF OZ.

Vivian Reed's heart is frozen by Old Mombi the witch (Mae Wells).

trous box office results. THE GREY NUN proved to be the company's final production. The Oz studio itself held out for a few months on rentals of stage space to other companies, but in the fall of 1915 the corporation was officially disbanded.

The acting in the Oz films is seen at its best in the antics of the various witches, Hottentots, and animals that hop and skip on and off the sets. This fact could in part be explained by the coincidence that Harold Lloyd and Hal Roach were among the extras at the Baum plant just prior to Roach's well-known inheritance that set him up as a producer. But it was the contribution of Fred Woodward, stalwart mule, kangaroo, and cowardly lion, which truly enlivened the films. Woodward had acted these roles in Baum's various flirtations with huge road-show theatrical presentations of the Oz stories, so he had, in a sense, grown into his characterizations. Other Baum actors included a very young Mildred Harris (usually playing little-boy roles) and Vivian Reed, the ''Oz Girl'' of the company trademark and pretty princess of most of the features.

It is unfair to compare Baum's primitive features with MGM's later Oz extravaganza in color (1939), but they are much more satisfying than such other outside ventures into Baum's lore as the Selig Oz pictures commissioned in 1908 for Baum's theatrical ''Radio Plays'' (actually an early mixed-media stage experiment, so titled before radio had been invented); or Larry Semon's 1925 rendition of THE WIZARD OF OZ in which Semon's rewrite of the old story to fit his clowning as well as his typical mid-twenties punning titles destroy much of the child-like flavor of the original work.

Baum's Oz novels will always be a part of the American cultural mythology, and it is fascinating to be able to view the filmed versions of these myths as Baum himself intended them to be seen.

Violet Macmillan, Pierre Coudere, and Frank Moore.

W. C. Fields returns home in IT'S THE OLD ARMY GAME, 1926.

In the old days that people call "good" and "halcyon," American entertainers had innumerable opportunities to develop their craft. Many, like Chaplin, started in vaudeville and perfected routines that the screen turned classic. The Marx Brothers toured the country before making a film and tried out their gags on live audiences. But some of the developing and much of the perfecting was done in films themselves. Rediscovered silent comedies made in the twenties by W. C. Fields—films like SO'S YOUR OLD MAN and IT'S THE OLD ARMY GAME—give a rare glimpse of a talent in transition, of Fields pulling himself together into studied anarchy. And in addition to their value as records of an artist-in-progress, the Fields silents offer another opportunity: to laugh.

Critic James Agee thought that W. C. Fields was "one of the funniest men on earth." A case could be made that he still is. The Fields comedies, often misunderstood or simply not understood at all in their own era, have become immensely popular in an age that thrives on anti-heroes. Overlooked, for the most part, in the great Fields renaissance have been his silent films. One reason they were overlooked is that some of them were lost. But now, titles like IT'S THE OLD ARMY GAME, one of his best, and SO'S YOUR OLD MAN—both made at Paramount in 1926—have been restored from their original negatives by The American Film Institute, while POOL SHARKS (Gaumount, 1915) and RUNNING WILD (Paramount, 1927) have been acquired for restoration.

Watching the silent Fields affords a new appreciation of his visual comic timing and inventiveness, a skill developed from vaudeville, where he started as a juggler. Not only are there the classic routines that he perfected on the stage—like the insane golf game of SO'S YOUR OLD MAN—but also the simple, casual, almost thrown-away sight gags that punctuate his performance in IT'S THE OLD ARMY GAME: shaking hands with a man while holding a lighted cigar, or awakening in a daze and putting both slippers on his left foot.

In some ways, the silent Fields films are like previews of works-in-progress. Fields in fact remade SO'S YOUR OLD MAN as YOU'RE TELLING ME in 1934 (with Larry "Buster" Crabbe as one of the young lovers). A few of the basic details were changed. In the first version, Samuel Bisbee (Fields) invents a shatter-proof windshield. In the second, it's a puncture-proof tire. But the stories are otherwise identical.

Bits of Fields business that worked in the silent films return again in the later sound features. The hilarious picnic on the lawn of a mansion in ARMY GAME was repeated in IT'S A GIFT (1934). Some of the situations that face druggist Elmer Prettywillie (Fields) in ARMY GAME come back to haunt druggist Dr. Dilweg in the 1933 Mack Sennett short, THE PHARMACIST. The classic IT'S A GIFT sequence in which Fields tries to sleep on one floor of a multi-tiered back porch, to be interrupted by children, ice-men, and somebody bellowing the name of "Carl LaFong," grew out of a similar but shorter sequence in ARMY GAME. Both end with Fields' own gunshot bringing about the collapse of the porch swing, with him on it.

The Fields silents also present us with a rougher, meaner version of the put-upon old reprobate. The ubiquitous Will Hays Production Code would later homogenize Fields, who would no longer be able to say "helluva" or to physically attack children with the vehemence he showed in ARMY GAME.

At one point in ARMY GAME he contemplates bashing his nephew with an axe. At another, he silences a baby with a blanket jammed into its mouth, then stuffs it in further with the handle of a fly-swatter. That doesn't quiet the baby, so he gives it a mallet and a mirror. The baby doesn't break the mirror but instead uses the mallet to conk Fields on the head (he's under the covers by then and does a poetic pain ballet—we can feel the agony without even being able to see his face). Fields considers dropping the baby off a balcony or throwing it into a garbage can. When he retracts a huge safety pin the child has swallowed, he tells the baby to "Kiss Uncle's head and make it well," but baby smashes a milk bottle over Fields' skull instead. Fields gives the safety pin back and, returning to his swing, calls out, "Uncle will give you some nice razor blades to play with."

W. C. Fields assays his shatter-proof windshield in SO'S YOUR OLD MAN, 1926.

Such violent encounters were toned down in the later sound films when censors and the Production Code became a constant nemesis to Fields.

IT'S THE OLD ARMY GAME was directed by Edward Sutherland. It begins with a title proclaiming sarcastically, "This is the epic of the American druggist." Fields, portraying Elmer Prettywillie, is introduced as "apothecary and humanitarian—ever ready to administer to those in distress." When the plot of ARMY GAME shows its face, many minutes into the film, it has something to do with a visiting con man and his landselling schemes, with which Fields gets briefly involved. There is also the obligatory love affair subplot between the con man and Louise Brooks. These subplots were usually inserted at studio insistence, and this one is dealt with as efficiently as possible.

Fields' enemy child in this picture is Mickey Bennett as, according to the titles, "Prettywillie's nephew ... a combination Peck's Bad Boy, Gyp the Blood, **169**

W. C. Fields.

One just wants change for a ten-dollar bill so he can make a phone call. Another wants a two-cent stamp, but not one from the edge of the sheet; he wants "one of those in the middle" (the man will return for another such stamp in THE PHARMACIST). Fields dutifully cuts it out and puts it in a bag. Then the phone rings—a customer wants to know if he will split a box of Smith Brothers cough drops and deliver it. Surprisingly, he refuses.

Another customer enters and asks for "something for the hip," meaning then-illegal alcohol. Before giving it to him, Fields produces a running fan from beneath the counter and with it blows the man's coat open. The man gets his hootch and departs. Later, another man will come in asking for liquor, and Fields will bring up the fan again. This time, we realize what he was doing with it—the lapels blow open to reveal a badge hidden on the vest beneath the coat. Fields delivers a hypocritical lecture on temperance and citizenship: "Would you have me break the laws of our glorious country to satisfy your depraved taste?"

As usual, Fields is about the only funny person in the film, but the titles do add some humor of their own, as when they observe that April Fool's Day is "a legal holiday in the Prettywillie household" or, earlier, philosophize that "Love at first sight saves a lot of time." The titles for SO'S YOUR OLD MAN are not funnier, but the descriptive, non-dialogue ones feature designs and drawings by John Held, Jr. whose work evokes the twenties as much, perhaps, as does any other artist's. In SO'S YOUR OLD MAN, Fields is again largely a hapless victim of vicious conspiracies. Like many comedies of the time, and for some years to come, the film is a put-down of the upper class, the social snob, the high-born and pompous, personified in this picture by old Mrs. A Brandewyne Murchison (Julia Ralph) who comes, she says, from "The Warrens of Virginia."

Fields, as Samuel Bisbee, glazier, is by contrast a poor man whom we first meet while he is in his undershirt tinkering with inventions in the garage. Fields played the role of Deflater of the Elite in many films; it is a comic tradition, of course. In this film his first words to Mrs. Murchison are, "I knew your old man

and Jesse James." The boy is of course a ruthless monster, but he is not the only threat to Fields. There is also just plain fate which conspires against him. When Fields goes to New York, it is not enough that he accidentally sets his car on fire and burns it to ashes. No, that could happen to anybody. When it happens to Fields, he also must take out his insurance policy, say how lucky it is the car's insured, and then watch as the policy blows out of his hand and into the fire, where it is naturally destroyed.

There are other adversaries. The customers who come into the drugstore spend little but demand much.

when he only had one pair of pants!''

SO'S YOUR OLD MAN is more preoccupied with plot than ARMY GAME, but it is still filled with great visual comedy by Fields, and it ends with the delightfully gratuitous golf sequence, in which the first stroke is delayed by, among other things: a rubber club that wobbles when swung; a caddy with some sticky paper; the sticky paper blowing back at Fields; Fields' stumble into a pie plate that sticks to his foot; the fact that the golf ball gets stuck to the end of a sticky club; and then a duck, struck by a wayward gunshot, that falls to the earth and of course knocks Fields to the ground.

Some of the jokes got better by the time they resurfaced in the remake. In OLD MAN, when Fields is anxious to placate his angry wife, he encounters a man outside a pet store who says, "I always take my wife pets" when she's upset. The man has bought a parrot. Fields goes into the store and emerges with a pony! In YOU'RE TELLING ME, it gets one step sillier. Fields hears the same advice and goes into the pet store, but this time he emerges with an ostrich. Getting it home is half the fun.

A more superficial intimation of things to come occurs in ARMY GAME, when Fields explains that film's title and also supplies the title of a future talkie. A visiting gambler has come to Fields' drugstore and is luring the crowd away from the land scheme with his find-the-pea-under-the-shell trick. Fields foils him; when challenged to find the pea, and knowing it isn't under any of the shells, he picks up the shells at both ends at once, leaving one in the middle. "It's under that one," he says, forcing the con man to either pay off or admit fraud. To the onlookers, Fields says, "It's the old Army game!" The hoax revealed, Fields offers some general counsel: "Never give a sucker an even break." It will be repeated in the "moral" at the end of the film and as the title of a 1941 comedy that Fields wanted to be called "The Great Man"—after himself.

The comic character created by W. C. Fields evolved through the silents and into the talkies with few substantial changes. Physically, Fields became fatter and

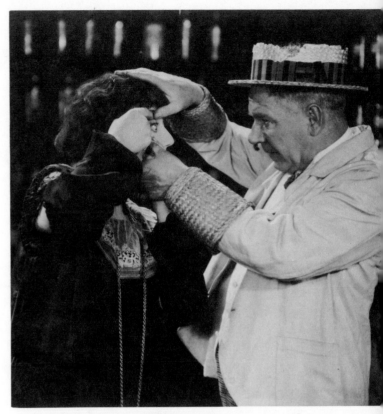

W. C. Fields performs a delicate operation in
IT'S THE OLD ARMY GAME.

his nose, always described as "bulbous," got bulbouser. The silly mustache tucked up high under his nose in OLD MAN actually hangs from the end of his nose, without apparent support from his lip, in ARMY GAME. It grew bigger and more realistic for HER MAJESTY, LOVE in 1931, but finally disappeared altogether for MILLION DOLLAR LEGS (1932).

At the end of SO'S YOUR OLD MAN, when all has presumably been set right in Fields' anarchic universe, the actress playing his daughter says, "I think my father is the funniest man in the world." The silent films of W. C. Fields give evidence that, like critic James Agee, she was both prescient and ahead of her time.

Frank Borzage

Burton J. Shapiro

Jack Curtis in UNTIL THEY GET ME, 1917.

Recovery and preservation of the films of Frank Borzage are helping to change his status from that of little-known director to renown as one of the creative forces in twenties and thirties cinema. Films like MAN'S CASTLE and LITTLE MAN, WHAT NOW? suggest that Borzage was a man of considerable talent, but it is the movies yet to be found and still to be preserved that may give Borzage the reputation he deserves.

Frank Borzage has always been known as the director of SEVENTH HEAVEN (1927) and a handful of other films usually seen in cut versions on a washed-out television screen. His visuals are soft and low-keyed, and each character, even the walk-ons, are such an integral part of his films, that any Borzage seen on television is only a ghost of the real thing. In its acquisition of a number of the important films of Borzage, ranging from the hitherto little-known UNTIL THEY GET ME (1917) to the more familiar SONG O' MY HEART (1930), MAN'S CASTLE (1933), LITTLE MAN, WHAT NOW? (1934), and DESIRE (1936), The American Film Institute has begun the work of preserving and restoring this director's films to their original state, making possible for the first time in thirty years a serious appraisal of Borzage's work.

Borzage the director was an excellent coordinator. In addition to his careful visual style, he was able to give added depth and understanding to his performers because of his own acting background. (Charles Farrell and Janet Gaynor were never again as good as they were in SEVENTH HEAVEN and STREET ANGEL, and Margaret Sullavan received much of her acclaim from her Borzage films.)

But Borzage was also a skillful story teller; more so, perhaps, because he was able to do so much with his one basic plot. This typical Borzage plot concerns two lovers who meet under mutual hardship or under what is to become hardship. Facing adversity together, they are often separated by outside forces until their lives are resolved when they overcome the flaws of the larger universe. This is the plot of SEVENTH HEAVEN, a sentimental film, and the forerunner of what seem to be numerous imitations by other direc-

172

tors. Borzage himself directed two remakes of this film for Fox: STREET ANGEL (1928) which suffers from an almost unbearable Germanic heaviness; and THE RIVER (1929), which was photographically more stunning than SEVENTH HEAVEN, though never able to achieve the audacious heights of the original. (Both of these films have been preserved by The Museum of Modern Art.)

Working for Columbia in 1933, Borzage made MAN'S CASTLE. Its story is similar to SEVENTH HEAVEN, only the setting is in New York's Lower East Side instead of the Paris slums. MAN'S CASTLE is remarkable in its building of character relationships. Perhaps one reason is Borzage's fantasy-like settings in the middle of the harshness of the real world, creating a kind of isolation in which the audience can empathize with the protagonists—a small world created solely for the couple caught in poverty. Using this confined space, Borzage manages to intertwine two personalities, the unemployed but proud and independent man and woman.

Extending this idea of a couple confined by uncontrollable circumstances is LITTLE MAN, WHAT NOW?, which Borzage made for Universal. In this film, the couple find themselves enmeshed in the early Nazi era in Germany. Their only recourse is each other. In an atmospheric sense, at least, there is a great similarity between the Hoover Flats of MAN'S CASTLE of 1933 and LITTLE MAN's Berlin of 1934. LITTLE MAN is also one of the first anti-Nazi films, and the beginning of Borzage's use of this motif which climaxes with THE MORTAL STORM (1940).

With the John McCormack vehicle, SONG O' MY HEART, Borzage proved his adeptness at handling material other than his own established genre. The American Film Institute, Fox, and The John McCormack Association of Greater Kansas City, Inc., restored the film, which was an attempt by Fox to find its own way through the 1929-1931 musical melange. Fox's Movietone (sound-on-film) method was far ahead of the Vitaphone system. To take advantage of the superior quality, Fox signed McCormack for a reputed sum of over $500,000 and then sent a crew, with Borzage as director, to Ireland. The film was a great success, and critics praised both the sound and

Loretta Young, Spencer Tracy, and Marjorie Rambeau in MAN'S CASTLE, 1933.

Hoover Flats in MAN'S CASTLE.

Marlene Dietrich and Gary Cooper in DESIRE, 1936.

the photography. Filmed in 70mm "Grandeur" with a well-engineered sound track, the film continues to look and sound impressive, and the Borzage feeling is evident throughout the sentimental sub-plot as well as in the cutaways from McCormack's singing.

DESIRE (made for Paramount) is a curious mixture of Borzage sentiment and Lubitsch (who produced the film) sophistication. It is a film reminiscent of TROUBLE IN PARADISE (1932) and bears almost no relation to any of Borzage's films either before or after 1936. (Possibly due to this collaboration on DESIRE between the two, Lubitsch seems to allude to Borzage's style in his later THE SHOP AROUND THE CORNER (1940) by blending much of his own style with a more somber romanticism, making SHOP more earnest than any of his other romantic comedies.)

Even more outside the Borzage plot line is his rare 1917 Western, UNTIL THEY GET ME. Unseen for about fifty years, this Triangle film was ground out with a characteristic "one-picture-a-week" story. Occasionally breaking through a plot about a murderer, a Royal Canadian Mounted policeman, and a poor orphan girl who runs away and finds romance, are some scenes that take on the atmosphere of his LAZY-BONES (1926) and SEVENTH HEAVEN. In one sequence of intense pathos, an Indian woman brings to the murderer his baby, and it is photographed in such a way—low-keyed and orange-tinted—that it is obvious that his wife has just died in childbirth. The muted quality of UNTIL THEY GET ME is also reminiscent of the doom foreshadowed prior to the shipwreck sequence in HISTORY IS MADE AT NIGHT (1937), which Borzage directed exactly twenty years later.

Although Borzage's total output has not yet been reclaimed, the films which are available prove that he is a director with many strengths and a quality and consistency that will be better known with the hoped-for acquisition of his remaining "lost" films.

Douglass Montgomery in LITTLE MAN, WHAT NOW?, 1934.

John McCormack in SONG O' MY HEART, 1930.

Tom Shales

THE LAST FLIGHT

First National Pictures. 1931.
Director: William Dieterle.
Screenplay: John Monk Saunders, based on his novel, *The Single La*
Cast: Richard Barthelmess, Johnny Mack Brown, Helen Chandler,
Walter Byron, Elliott Nugent, David Manners.

Film history or history on film? Sometimes the two melt into one another. THE LAST FLIGHT is a fictional film, made after the decade it depicts, but it survives now as one of the few cinematic translations of The Lost Generation. Further, in expressing the disillusion and flippant anxiety of that era, it begins to exhibit the same demeanor, so that where the portrayal ends and the documentary begins becomes a point not easy to discern. THE LAST FLIGHT is a revealing and a very significant oddball.

Gertrude Stein proclaimed it "The Lost Generation" and F. Scott Fitzgerald kept its diary. Lesser known is the fact that William Dieterle put it on film in 1931 in a recklessly oddball movie called THE LAST FLIGHT.

The film is an unmistakable evocation of post-war orphans and their witty dissipation. Compared with other films of its time, it is strange indeed. The screenplay, by John Monk Saunders from his novel *The Single Lady,* is determinedly sophisticated, full of Mad-Hatter dialogue and characters about whom we are told precious little. It concentrates on four World War I fighter pilots who have been stranded by the armistice. There is no tangible plot to the film, although things do happen. Two of the flyers lose their lives in ways that are almost comical in their irrelevance to central circumstances. (One, for instance, foolishly hops into a bull ring, where he is fatally injured. Before dying, he explains his action with the classic existentialistic phrase, "It seemed like a good idea at the time.") Another one of the flyers shoots a man and vanishes into the night, thereby killing off the movie's one character of apparent purpose. He was named Frink; the purposes he had were usually libidinous or corrupt, and he refused to view life as a pointless charade—which puts him in the minority when surrounded by the flyers and the girl they casually adopted.

Amorality seems in the air, yet when the four pilots discover the girl, Nikki (Helen Chandler), standing in a nightclub holding a champagne glass with a set of dentures in it (forty years before A CLOCKWORK ORANGE, as it happens), they latch onto her, not apparently in the hope of sexual communion, but because they recognize she shares their flippant isolationism and the sense that life is pointless.

The film begins with furious air battle footage borrowed from THE DAWN PATROL (1930). The frenzy of it is in sharp contrast to the rest of the film, although director William Dieterle never lets things get lazy. The characters may be lost, but the director isn't. The absence of traditional narrative structure doesn't really become apparent until, perhaps, the middle of the film. It leaves the audience stranded in much the same way as the pilots are. One of Dieterle's neatest touches is a slow dissolve after the battle footage, from a propeller gradually winding down to a meandering clock. Visually, it's effective, and it symbolizes the basic dilemma of the pilots. Richard Barthelmess as Cary Lockwood and David Manners as Shep Lambert leave the hospital that battle has sent them to in good spirits, of sorts. "Well," says Lockwood, "the old *guerre* is *finie.*" And what to do now? He has an answer: "Get tight and stay tight."

An old doctor watches them leave, however, and intones a grim benediction: "Well, there they go, out to face life—and their whole training was in preparation for death." He compares them to "spent bullets . . . shattered watches" and says they are "cooled off . . . useless. . . ." Then it is Paris, 1919, and Claridge's, where the two pilots and their two pals make an eager foursome when it's time to order drinks: "Martini! Martini! Martini! Martini!" The dialogue becomes fast and sassy and includes such phrases as "whole helluva lot" and this exchange:

Nikki: "I don't let anyone kiss me, hard."

Cary: "We'll let that pass."

The girl is essentially a sophisticated innocent—a lost one, of course. We are not told where she and the four pilots get the money that allows them a life of steady drinking, usually in formal wear. Richard Barthelmess is the most enigmatic of the four. In a tux and a big white twenties hat, he looks great, the soul of a soulless age. Perhaps never before nor since have those longing—even aching—eyes been put to such good use in a role. They stare out into emptiness or shift with anxious suspicion. During a closing

Richard Barthelmess, Johnny Mack Brown, Elliott Nugent, David Manners, and Helen Chandler in THE LAST FLIGHT.

*Richard Barthelmess, Elliott Nugent, Johnny Mack Brown,
Yola d'Auril, Walter Byron, David Manners, and
Helen Chandler in THE LAST FLIGHT.*

scene, when pal Shep Lambert is dying in the back seat of a car, Lockwood orders the driver to stop. Ironically, the car stops just in front of a carousel, which continues its merry and oblivious whirl. Shep dies and Lockwood searches for some vestige of reason in all this, at the same time refusing to succumb to relatively easy tears. It is one of the film's fine moments.

Earlier, Lockwood goes quietly to the popular French gravesite of Abelard and Heloise, the legendary lovers. Nikki follows him. There is little explanation in the script as to why this place holds such meaning for Lockwood but, again, the eyes suggest a great deal. It is here that, after Lockwood tells a euphemized version of the Abelard and Heloise tale, Nikki will suffer her one emotional moment in the film. She tells Cary, "Nothing can touch you! You're lost! You're all lost!" and the theme is articulated again.

The director so cleverly avoids the static and theatrical that an overwritten script fails to slow the movie or turn it detrimentally languid. It moves. In the first half, there are several scenes of the five revellers at a table. Dieterle shows imagination and initiative at photographing these sessions. He keeps the camera active—not hyperactive, but active—moving in on individuals and moving out again, not to give dramatic emphasis to what they say, but on a sort of arbitrary basis, wisely in keeping with the screenplay and its avoidance of emotional climax in the severely structured scene. It is, we might say, an amoral way of shooting a picture. Here, it works. There can be no emotionalism beyond the devil-may-care attitude of the characters, and there isn't. Even Frank's comic-opera seduction of Nikki (which fails, of course), and Lockwood's sock to the Frink jaw are dealt with dispassionately, at least as compared to other films of the period.

Later, bullfight footage is intercut with shots of the principals in a studio grandstand. When Talbot leaps into the ring, he is fatally gored by the bull. His dying scene is done without histrionics and with some humor ("a good idea at the time"). When Shep dies a short time later, he seems glad: "It's just like we're falling!" he shouts, and the implication is that he should have—in fact, did—die in a crash during the war. The film does not stop for much mourning, however. Even its most dramatic scene, the one in the graveyard, ends with an out-of-the-blue *non sequitur*: "I wonder what's happening in Portugal tonight."

Finally, Cary and Nikki find themselves on a train, bound for, naturally, they know not where, or, if they do, they care not where. Some semblance of a relationship has formed between them. At least they have their own survival in common. "What can I get you?" asks Cary. "What do you want?" "Well," says Nikki, "I've always wanted a pair of Spanish earrings." The train disappears into the distance. That is the end. THE LAST FLIGHT is an incomparably charismatic film and anything but ordinary. It gives a look into an era and a life style that is unique for the medium.

Index of Film Titles and Film Makers

Photograph Sources